T
EVERYDAY
GUIDE TO...
THE PROVERBS

THE
EVERYDAY
GUIDE TO...
THE PROVERBS

PAUL M. MILLER

HUMBLECREEK
INSPIRATION FOR LIFE

© 2005 by Barbour Publishing, Inc.

ISBN 1-59310-727-7

All rights reserved. No part of this publication may be reproduced or transmitted for commercial purposes, except for brief quotations in printed reviews, without written permission of the publisher.

Churches and other noncommercial interests may reproduce portions of this book without the express written permission of Humble Creek, provided that the text does not exceed 500 words or 5 percent of the entire book, whichever is less, and that the text is not material quoted from another publisher. When reproducing text from this book, include the following credit line: "From *The Everyday Guide to the Proverbs*, published by Humble Creek. Used by permission."

All scripture quotations, unless otherwise noted, are taken from the King James Version of the Bible.

Scripture quotations marked NKJV are taken from the New King James Version. Copyright © 1979, 1980, 1982 by Thomas Nelson, Inc. Used by permission. All rights reserved.

Published by Humble Creek, P.O. Box 719, Uhrichsville, Ohio 44683

Printed in the United States of America.
5 4 3 2 1

Contents

Introduction

A Word to the Want-to-Be Wise

We have heard them all our lives: "A penny saved is a penny earned; A stitch in time saves nine; A rolling stone gathers no moss." By now, we have figured out that these aphorisms are trying to remind us of life's truth. They are clever ways of nudging and teaching "This is the way to happiness."

Long before Ben Franklin penned his first homely truism in *Poor Richard's Almanac*, King Solomon and his fellow proverb scribes realized that humankind needed gentle nudges and straightforward instruction in the practical issues of life. While not written on tablets of stone, the Old Testament book we call "The Proverbs of Solomon" has at its heart the basic instructions that will lead to wisdom, justice, judgment, and equity (Proverbs 1:3).

To the wisest man that the world had ever known, wisdom is the foundation of happiness. Today we attempt to impart to our children the so-called "smarts" that will make their worlds stay on course. At one stage, it's "Use a fork instead of your fingers." At another, it's "Don't be too proud of yourself; the folks around you may have something to laugh at." And at a third, it's "Have truthful lips; they can make life so much easier."

Frankly, while written for all people everywhere, King Solomon's "apples of gold" are particularly targeted to youth. There is not an adolescent or young adult anywhere who would not benefit from the thirty-one brief divisions of Solomon's "best-seller." These wise sayings about the practical affairs of everyday life reflect the author's passion for knowledge and wisdom. Even as a young man he was consumed with realizing their importance in his life (1 Kings 3:9–12).

Building upon the attributes of knowledge and wisdom, Solomon became something of a literary prodigy. It is said that kings came to hear him, and he mastered science, politics, business, poetry, ethics, and expounding God's truth (1 Kings 4 and 9). The man must even have had something of a sense of humor: "Even a fool, when he holdeth his peace, is counted wise" (17:28); "It is better to dwell in a corner of the housetop, than with a brawling woman in a wide house" (21:9); and his description of an imbiber who's had too much wine (23:31–35) is wonderfully descriptive!

Sharpen Your Wits. . .
For the next thirteen weeks you will be involved in a study of Solomon's Proverbs. While not an in-depth study, it will confront you with what a divinely-inspired thinker holds up as universal truth. As a help to your understanding of the material, consider these suggestions:

- Always begin your study time with prayer. Ask the Lord to make clear His will for you through the words of the day's scripture passage.

- Spend reflective time comparing the wise words to your own life. Use this study for your personal spiritual growth.

- Keep a notebook handy to record your personal reactions to each selection you read.

- Consider reading the daily Proverbs scripture selection in another version, along with the King James Version provided.

- Consider writing a personal paraphrase of a key verse in the selection. Make it applicable to your needs and situation.

- Work at memorizing a key verse in each day's selection.

- Share what you've discovered with a family member or friend.

"The fear of the LORD is the beginning of knowledge" (Proverbs 1:7).

PAUL M. MILLER

Week One

If you are looking for meditative, "feel good" scripture readings, the book of Proverbs may not be the selection for you. But if you're seeking direction for your life, along with the ability to properly relate to people around you, to overcome bad habits, to add depth to your understanding, to learn the difference between "smarts" and wisdom, to please the One who created you—then you are about to undertake what just may be the best thirteen weeks of your life!

Proverbs is a part of the Old Testament that holds what is called "wisdom literature." This classification is usually given to the books of Job, Psalms, Proverbs, Ecclesiastes, and the Song of Solomon. They are generally instructive and poetic, and they have a very special place in Jewish teaching.

The Hebrew word translated "proverbs" is also translated "taut" in other places. This is certainly a picture of the purpose of any proverb: It is truth expressed with as few words as possible. These wise sayings are spare, lean, to the point, instructive, and often expressed with passion in figurative language. They were meant to grab the attention of the person on the street or dozing in a pew (though the Jews usually stood during worship).

Authorship cannot be pinpointed to a single contributor—not even Solomon. Some of the book's content has been traced to pre-Solomon times, other portions to many other sources. For the sake of simplicity, this writer will assign authorship to Solomon throughout.

The Proverbs, we discover, are written in the first-person voice. Generally the "I" and "me" refers to Solomon and the other writers. There are times, though, when the "I" sounds more like God than a human teacher. Note that the name *God* or its equivalent does not appear often in the book. Actually, the tone of 1:15–19 and other references sounds more like a heartbroken father, whose guidance has been cast aside by a willful son or daughter. The father in Jesus' parable that we call "The Prodigal Son" (Luke 15) could easily have spoken these exact words—as could a Father in heaven who has been so disappointed in His creation.

A Page from Contemporary Life

There was no punishment for my son Timmy quite as earthshaking as saying, "Son, why are you acting like a baby?" Since our child rearing was "Spockian," we had to forget the "Spare the rod and spoil the child" admonition and find less traumatizing discipline. Accusing Timmy of babyish behavior was enough to remind him to behave responsibly for a full day—sometimes.

As he got older, and we substituted Tim for Timmy, I also substituted the word *immature* for "like a baby." Above all else, our son wanted to be thought of as mature. As every parent knows, every kid has his moments of silliness and thoughtlessness—don't we all? But we often talked about the patterns of his life. He was very proud of his report cards, and he did reasonably well in school. But at one particular Parents' Night, his teacher, who really cared for Tim, said, "Tim could be an even better student if he'd start thinking before he 'leaps.' "

Those comments from Tim's teacher caused a long conversation about the difference between being smart and having wisdom. To this day, my son, who is a man well into his career, remembers that conversation. He says it was the beginning of a turning point for him. Wisdom doesn't necessarily show up on a report card, but is evident in the maturity of our relationships and decisions.

DAY 1

Proverbs 1:1–9

1 The proverbs of Solomon the son of David, king of Israel;

2 To know wisdom and instruction; to perceive the words of understanding;

3 To receive the instruction of wisdom, justice, and judgment, and equity;

4 To give subtilty to the simple, to the young man knowledge and discretion.

5 A wise man will hear, and will increase learning; and a man of understanding shall attain unto wise counsels:

6 To understand a proverb, and the interpretation; the words of the wise, and their dark sayings.

7 The fear of the LORD is the beginning of knowledge: but fools despise wisdom and instruction.

8 My son, hear the instruction of thy father, and forsake not the law of thy mother:

9 For they shall be an ornament of grace unto thy head, and chains about thy neck.

Reflecting on Proverbs 1:1–9

Meaning, please. . .

equity (1:3) just and fair

subtilty (or subtlety) (1:4) shrewdness

ornament of grace (1:9) garland of flowers

Read and React

Just as contemporary teachers are aware of the importance of practical truth, so were Solomon and his fellow writers/compilers. For them, practical truth was found in this tenth-century BC collection of proverbs. To help readers of that day grasp the divine scope of this anthology, it was necessary to provide a succinct preview of what awaited the reader—thus, the statement of origin, purpose, and theme (1:1–9).

From whom else in the tenth century BC would you expect such a book? It had to originate from the "wisest man in all the world."

____ Who might you expect to write the book of Proverbs today?

King David's son, Solomon, was convinced that these truths were beneficial for the smooth running of not only a nation, but also a family and each individual within that family. This, for him, was the rudimentary reason for providing his world with this information.

____ If you were updating this purpose statement, what would you add that isn't there now?

____ Verse 3: "Wisdom, justice, judgment, and equity" are four facets of life that ought to be clearly demonstrated in the lives of men and women today. How would each of these traits or characteristics affect your life? How would they affect the world?

____ Verse 4: "Knowledge and discretion." The young are singled out to receive knowledge and discretion. This is so appropriate. It takes knowledge to help a young man or woman be discreet in their words and actions. What is discretion? When is it important? What has been the result when you have failed to exercise it?

____ Verse 8: This verse falls under the topic of embracing wisdom. Notice the assignment given to fathers (instruction) and mothers (law). Does it sound like the mother is expected to be the disciplinarian? One commentary suggests that the father's task is to prepare the child for his place in the world, while the mother is the child's teacher. Reflect on this in your role as a parent and as a child.

Take Inventory

• What paths do you need to keep away from?

• Regarding members of your family, what are their potential slippery slopes? How can you be a voice of reason for them?

To Memorize

The fear of the LORD is the beginning of knowledge. Proverbs 1:7

• • •

DAY 2

Proverbs 1:10–23

10 My son, if sinners entice thee, consent thou not.

11 If they say, Come with us, let us lay wait for blood, let us lurk privily for the innocent without cause:

12 Let us swallow them up alive as the grave; and whole, as those that go down into the pit:

13 We shall find all precious substance, we shall fill our houses with spoil:

14 Cast in thy lot among us; let us all have one purse:

15 My son, walk not thou in the way with them; refrain thy foot from their path:

16 For their feet run to evil, and make haste to shed blood.

17 Surely in vain the net is spread in the sight of any bird.

18 And they lay wait for their own blood; they lurk privily for their own lives.

19 So are the ways of every one that is greedy of gain; which taketh away the life of the owners thereof.

20 Wisdom crieth without; she uttereth her voice in the streets:

21 She crieth in the chief place of concourse, in the openings of the gates: in the city she uttereth her words, saying,

22 How long, ye simple ones, will ye love simplicity? and the scorners delight in their scorning, and fools hate knowledge?

23 Turn you at my reproof: behold, I will pour out my spirit unto you, I will make known my words unto you.

Reflecting on Proverbs 1:10–23

Meaning, please. . .

privily (1:11) privately

spoil (1:13) plunder

lot, purse (1:14) belongings, finances

concourse (1:21) public square

simplicity (1:22) simple ways

scorners (1:22) mockers

reproof (1:23) rebuke

spirit (1:23) heart

Read and React

Reading further into Proverbs, we are still moved by the author's fatherly way of writing. A word to a parent: Regardless of your importance, schedule, hobbies, etc., your number one assignment is to be a parent to your child. Hide these words in your heart to infiltrate your guidance and direction.

____ Verses 10–14: What a vivid description of the cunning enticements that evildoers toss out to the unwary. Their words excite the ego and play upon one's natural desire for possessions and importance. Their temptations promise the unwise child that he shall be part of a group that will care for his needs. How does the Evil One tempt today? Are there common denominators?

____ Verse 20: Wisdom is portrayed with great passion in this verse. Interestingly, wisdom is personified with a female pronoun. This is probably a carryover from the Greek culture, in which the refined characteristics are given female attributes. In other words, there is beauty in wisdom.

So, what is Wisdom so worked up about? Why is she so free in delivering her message? It's because she knows that when we accept truth (wisdom), it will set us free!

___ Verse 22: To our writer, it is obvious that even the simpleminded and those who make fun of faith can receive wisdom. Think about how wisdom relates to your life. You may not be a fool or a mocker, but do others see wisdom radiating from your life?

Take Inventory

• Does your school and book knowledge involve your heart?

• When you have involved your heart in discovering information, has it become knowledge? How?

• If wisdom involves the heart, how does this affect relationships within the family, with friends, and at work?

To Memorize

I will pour out my spirit heart unto you. I will make known my words unto you. Proverbs 1:23

• • •

Day 3

Proverbs 1:24–33
24 Because I have called, and ye refused; I have stretched out my hand, and no man regarded;

25 But ye have set at nought all my counsel, and would none of my reproof:

26 I also will laugh at your calamity; I will mock when your fear cometh;

27 When your fear cometh as desolation, and your destruction cometh as a whirlwind; when distress and anguish cometh upon you.

28 Then shall they call upon me, but I will not answer; they shall seek me early, but they shall not find me:

29 For that they hated knowledge, and did not choose the fear of the LORD:

30 They would none of my counsel: they despised all my reproof.

31 Therefore shall they eat of the fruit of their own way, and be filled with their own devices.

32 For the turning away of the simple shall slay them, and the prosperity of fools shall destroy them.

33 But whoso hearkeneth unto me shall dwell safely, and shall be quiet from fear of evil.

Reflecting on Proverbs 1:24–33

Meaning, please. . .

laugh (1:26) not heartlessness, but reaction to how absurd those are who turn her down

counsel, reproof (1:30) advice, rebuke

Read and React

As was already mentioned, the word *God* or its equivalent appears sparingly in Proverbs. This has puzzled scholars and readers alike. For we who live in light of New Testament teaching, it may seem strange to personify wisdom instead of offering God's hand or His Son, Jesus, in time of trouble. No need to doubt! You will remember, these are homey reminders of what comprises maturity, written in a literary style of its day. It is not a theological statement of doctrine.

____ Verse 27: These are graphic words: *fear, desolation, destruction, distress, anguish.* Lady Wisdom doesn't promise her children an escape from these calamities, but she does promise that her hand will be available in the midst of them. Reflect on wisdom as a help in time of trouble. How is heart wisdom different from being smart? What does it have to offer in troubled times?

____ Verse 30: There is something headstrong about those who hate advice. In Jesus' day there were those who were called "stiff-necked." They were the know-it-alls who spurned what Jesus had to say. Isn't it the emotionally and spiritually mature person who is able to accept instruction and advice? Pray about that as in issue in your own life.

____ Verse 33: For you who will listen, Lady Wisdom is right there with a promise: "Whoso hearkeneth unto me shall dwell safely, and shall be quiet from fear of evil." Your homework for today is to restate this promise in a contemporary and more personalized way.

Take Inventory
• Son or daughter, think what you are accepting when you receive His words and commandments.

• Consider how your life might change if you accept His words and commandments.

• What would your marks of maturity be?

To Memorize
Whoso hearkeneth unto me shall dwell safely and shall be quiet from fear of evil. Proverbs 1:33

DAY 4

Proverbs 2:1–9

1 My son, if thou wilt receive my words, and hide my commandments with thee;

2 So that thou incline thine ear unto wisdom, and apply thine heart to understanding;

3 Yea, if thou criest after knowledge, and liftest up thy voice for understanding;

4 If thou seekest her as silver, and searchest for her as for hid treasures;

5 Then shalt thou understand the fear of the LORD, and find the knowledge of God.

6 For the LORD giveth wisdom: out of his mouth cometh knowledge and understanding.

7 He layeth up sound wisdom for the righteous: he is a buckler to them that walk uprightly.

8 He keepeth the paths of judgment, and preserveth the way of his saints.

9 Then shalt thou understand righteousness, and judgment, and equity; yea, every good path.

Reflecting on Proverbs 2:1–9

Meaning, please. . .

buckler (2:7) a shield

Read and React

In Proverbs 1, Solomon exhorts us to embrace wisdom and warns us against rejecting wisdom. Here in chapter 2, we are presented with the moral benefits of acquiring and practicing wisdom.

The text is full of active words, verbs, if you please. The first four verses include these, set in modern English: *receive, hide, incline, apply, cry, lift, seek, search, understand, find.*

When set into the frame of wisdom, these ten verbs underscore Lady

Wisdom's formula for acquiring wisdom, which in turn, perfects maturity. They are very nearly a progression to claiming wisdom and maturity for yourself.

___ Verses 1–2: Consider each of these phrases: *Receive my words.* Her words have been a plea to acquire wisdom. *Hide my commandments.* She urges us to store away what she has commanded. *Incline your ear to wisdom.* Tune your mind to hearing wisdom. *Apply your heart to be understanding.* Maturity requires an understanding heart.

___ Verses 3–4: *Cry out for knowledge.* Become desperate for mature wisdom. *Lift up your voice and ask for understanding.* Don't be shy in your search. *Seek or look for wisdom as you would silver.* Be on the lookout for every opportunity to gain spiritual maturity. *Search for wisdom as you would for buried treasure.* Discovering treasure has a huge reward—so does finding wisdom.

And the huge reward for all this action?

___ Verse 5: According to what you have just read, you will understand the fear of the Lord. The Lord is scared? No, it means you are in awe of Him; you have come to an understanding of how great He is. Fear and awe are the same in this poetic language.

When you discover the knowledge of God, that is, to understand that He gives wisdom, then you will understand what is right and good and just—the paths that mature men and women take. Those are the benefits of accepting mature wisdom.

Take Inventory

• Son or daughter, think what you are accepting when you receive His words and commandments.

• Consider how your life might change if you accept His words and commandments.

• What verbs describe your hunger for maturity?

You hear so many voices in your day, how can you single out the voice of God?

Based on the old school grading system (A, B, C, D, F), what grade would Lady Wisdom give your emotional and spiritual maturity?

To Memorize
He keepeth the paths of judgment, and preserveth the way of his saints. Proverbs 2:8

. . .

Day 5

Proverbs 2:10–22
10 When wisdom entereth into thine heart, and knowledge is pleasant unto thy soul;
   11 Discretion shall preserve thee, understanding shall keep thee:
   12 To deliver thee from the way of the evil man, from the man that speaketh froward things;
   13 Who leave the paths of uprightness, to walk in the ways of darkness;
   14 Who rejoice to do evil, and delight in the frowardness of the wicked;
   15 Whose ways are crooked, and they froward in their paths:
   16 To deliver thee from the strange woman, even from the stranger which flattereth with her words;
   17 Which forsaketh the guide of her youth, and forgetteth the covenant of her God.
   18 For her house inclineth unto death, and her paths unto the dead.
   19 None that go unto her return again, neither take they hold of the paths of life.
   20 That thou mayest walk in the way of good men, and keep the paths of the righteous.
   21 For the upright shall dwell in the land, and the perfect shall remain in it.

22 But the wicked shall be cut off from the earth, and the transgressors shall be rooted out of it.

Reflecting on Proverbs 2:10–22

Meaning, please. . .

speaketh froward things (2:12) speak perverse things

paths of uprightness (2:13) straight paths

froward in their paths (2:15) devious in the ways

strange woman (2:16) adulteress or wayward wife

guide of her youth (2:17) partner of her youth

her house inclineth unto death (2:18) going into her house leads to death

Read and React

At this point in Proverbs, we have temporarily moved away from the concept of Lady Wisdom and are now perceiving the attribute of wisdom as something more personally given by God. This block of Proverbs continues with the listing of benefits derived from pursuing wisdom. This includes *discretion, understanding,* and *deliverance.*

___ Verse 10: Here it is again, the word *wisdom.* According to Solomon, this gift of wisdom will enter your heart. Again, the difference between *wisdom* and *smarts.* Authentic wisdom takes root in the heart because, according to scripture, that is the location of understanding and affection. Ah, the secret of wisdom includes affection. Why is that important?

___ Verse 10: Now, the contrasting word *knowledge.* It is "pleasant to your soul." It gives great satisfaction. In another place, it is described as "sweet."

___ Verse 11: Here is *discretion* again. It will preserve us. Preservation in the Old Testament does not mean we are placed in a jar of formaldehyde or given a jar of cream that will keep us forever young. No, to be preserved by God is a promise that we will be kept close to His great heart; we will be protected. We will be made fit for heaven; we have received His promise of eternal life.

Take Inventory

• The simile of life as a path is prevalent throughout Proverbs—throughout all scripture. Where is your path headed? Proverbs 2:13 implies that it is possible to be enticed off the path of uprightness and then to find oneself in darkness. You remember childhood stories about kids who leave the path through the woods and then find themselves in trouble? That's not just a fairy tale—perhaps you or someone you care for is facing that dilemma right now. Pray for deliverance and direction.

To Memorize

When wisdom entereth into thine heart, and knowledge is pleasant unto thy soul. Proverbs 2:10

. . .

DAY 6

Proverbs 3:1–20

1 My son, forget not my law; but let thine heart keep my commandments:

2 For length of days, and long life, and peace, shall they add to thee.

3 Let not mercy and truth forsake thee: bind them about thy neck; write them upon the table of thine heart:

4 So shalt thou find favour and good understanding in the sight of God and man.

5 Trust in the LORD with all thine heart; and lean not unto thine own understanding.

6 In all thy ways acknowledge him, and he shall direct thy paths.

7 Be not wise in thine own eyes: fear the LORD, and depart from evil.

8 It shall be health to thy navel, and marrow to thy bones.

9 Honour the LORD with thy substance, and with the firstfruits of all thine increase:

10 So shall thy barns be filled with plenty, and thy presses shall burst out with new wine.

11 My son, despise not the chastening of the LORD; neither be weary of his correction:

12 For whom the LORD loveth he correcteth; even as a father the son in whom he delighteth.

13 Happy is the man that findeth wisdom, and the man that getteth understanding.

14 For the merchandise of it is better than the merchandise of silver, and the gain thereof than fine gold.

15 She is more precious than rubies: and all the things thou canst desire are not to be compared unto her.

16 Length of days is in her right hand; and in her left hand riches and honour.

17 Her ways are ways of pleasantness, and all her paths are peace.

18 She is a tree of life to them that lay hold upon her: and happy is every one that retaineth her.

19 The LORD by wisdom hath founded the earth; by understanding hath he established the heavens.

20 By his knowledge the depths are broken up, and the clouds drop down the dew.

Reflecting on Proverbs 3:1–20

Meaning, please. . .

bind them about thy neck (3:3) implies the scriptures Jews wore on their bodies

health to thy navel (3:8) health to your body

marrow to thy bones (3:8) nourishment to your bones

merchandise (3:14) profit

Read and React

Proverbs continues to make wisdom a desirable attribute for life by heaping benefit upon benefit to it. The father to son dialogue continues, too. He holds out such a great promise: It is possible to win favor and a good name in the eyes of God and mankind (3:4). How?

According to 3:1, it's possible by never forgetting God's law and by keeping His commandments in your heart. The benefits? Long life, peace, mercy, truth, favor, good understanding, and godly direction (3:1–10).

The two verses in this passage that have been memorized by believers everywhere are Proverbs 3:5 and 3:6, "Trust in the LORD with all thine heart; and lean not unto thine own understanding. In all thy ways acknowledge him, and he shall direct thy paths."

___Verse 5: When seeking direction, *trust* is the key word. You can trust maps, atlases, and compasses to help you on the highway. But most of us need direction for other dimensions of our lives. Maps won't work. How are you at trusting in the Lord?

___Verse 6: *All* doesn't provide much wiggle room for exceptions. "All your ways" might be retranslated "the totality of your life." That's everything that is you.

Take Inventory

• In your quiet time, wrestle with the word *acknowledge*. Consider the extent of how you are mindful of God's presence in your daily life. A wonderful disciple named Paul Martin once said, "Live your life as if you wouldn't be surprised to run into Jesus as you walked around the corner."

• Consider, too, how willing and faithful your heart is to Him as you serve Him.

Trust in the LORD with all thine heart; and lean not unto thine own understanding. In all thy ways acknowledge him, and he shall direct thy paths. Proverbs 3:5–6

. . .

DAY 7

Proverbs 3:21–35

21 My son, let not them depart from thine eyes: keep sound wisdom and discretion:

22 So shall they be life unto thy soul, and grace to thy neck.

23 Then shalt thou walk in thy way safely, and thy foot shall not stumble.

24 When thou liest down, thou shalt not be afraid: yea, thou shalt lie down, and thy sleep shall be sweet.

25 Be not afraid of sudden fear, neither of the desolation of the wicked, when it cometh.

26 For the LORD shall be thy confidence, and shall keep thy foot from being taken.

27 Withhold not good from them to whom it is due, when it is in the power of thine hand to do it.

28 Say not unto thy neighbour, Go, and come again, and to morrow I will give; when thou hast it by thee.

29 Devise not evil against thy neighbour, seeing he dwelleth securely by thee.

30 Strive not with a man without cause, if he have done thee no harm.

31 Envy thou not the oppressor, and choose none of his ways.

32 For the froward is abomination to the LORD: but his secret is with the righteous.

33 The curse of the LORD is in the house of the wicked: but he blesseth the habitation of the just.

34 Surely he scorneth the scorners: but he giveth grace unto the lowly.

35 The wise shall inherit glory: but shame shall be the promotion of fools.

Meaning, please. . .

afraid of sudden fear (3:25) fear of sudden disaster

desolation of the wicked (3:25) the ruin that overtakes the wicked

foot taken (3:26) foot in a trap

his secret (3:32) his confidence

Read and React

President Franklin Roosevelt, during World War 2, declared, "We have nothing to fear, but fear itself." What would FDR say to us today, in the shadow of 9/11? We do have something to fear. No one in his right mind can pass off the dark specters that loiter around the edges of today's newspapers.

Did Solomon have his own brand of terrorists and Middle East disasters? In these verses (3:23–25), he is moved to speak unequivocally of fear. "You shall walk in the way safely. . .your foot shall not stumble. . . you shall not be afraid to lie down. . .you shall not fear some sudden disaster."

___ Verse 26: What place does fear have in the life of a maturing believer? In your life?

Stop your trembling. "The Lord will be your confidence, and shall keep your foot from being trapped." Now, read what Saint Teresa of Avila has to say about fear:

> *Let nothing disturb thee,*
> *Nothing afright thee;*
> *All things are passing;*
> *God never changeth.*

___Verse 27: When we have finally conquered fear, and our timidity is under control, Solomon reminds his readers that the courageous believer has a responsibility to his community: "Withhold not good from them to whom it is due, when it is in power of thine hand to do it." There is an implication here, though not spelled out, that nudges the newly freed believer to bear concern for the needs of those less fortunate. Do good.

Take Inventory

• Take a piece of paper and a pencil and make a list of any fears that may linger around the edges of your life. Next, scratch off the list all those fears that are absolutely unfounded. Then turn anything that's left over to God.

To Memorize

Withhold not good from them to whom it is due, when it is in the power of thine hand to do it. Proverbs 3:27

WEEK TWO
PROVERBS 4, 5, 6, AND 7

What more could Solomon and his fellow contributors have to say to us? We plowed through some pretty heavy topics last week. Much of the material held up all the reasons why we should pursue wisdom. In addition, there were rather realistic warnings about using our wisdom to keep pure in our relationships.

Now we roll up our sleeves and dig into how we obtain wisdom (chapter 4), another lesson on unchastity (chapter 5), naughtiness and idleness (chapter 6), and the dangers of adultery (chapter 7). If there seems to be repetition in the Proverbs subject matter, accept the fact that the sin of immorality has continuously been a blight on humanity.

Solomon is not the subject of many poems, but here's one. Read it several times, and overlook the seeming negativity. It does speak to today, and it will be referred to during this week.

Gone in the Wind

Solomon! Where is thy throne? It is gone in the wind.
Babylon! Where is thy might? It is gone in the wind.
Like the swift shadows of Noon, like the dreams of the Blind,
Vanish the glories and pomp of the earth in the wind.

Man! Canst thou build upon aught in the pride of thy mind?
Wisdom will teach thee that nothing can tarry behind;
Though there be thousand bright actions embalmed
*   and enshrined,*
Myriads and millions of brighter are snow in the wind.

Solomon! Where is thy throne? It is gone in the wind.
Babylon! Where is thy might? It is gone in the wind.
All that the genius of Man hath achieved and designed
Waits for it's hour to be dealt with as dust by the wind.

Pity thou, reader! The madness of poor humankind,
Raving of Knowledge,—and Satan so busy to blind!
Raving of Glory,—like me,—for the garlands I bind
(Garlands of song) are but gathered, and—strewn in the wind!

—JAMES CLARENCE MANGAN, 1803–1849

A Page from Contemporary Life

Sometimes a person will make a suggestion or even offer a criticism that at the time will cut to the quick, but then over the years it returns again and again, and in our realistic moments we admit the truth in what was spoken.

So it was during my senior year in college. If you had asked me, I would have quickly told you, "Wisdom? I've got it! Take a look at my transcript. I'm on my way to graduate school in Berkeley." How dare anyone question my intellect or sophistication!

Then one day on a blue-skied, pre-smog Southern California afternoon, I was rushing up the Ad Building stairs two at a time, when a Dr. Cecil Miller (no relation) put himself right in front of me and asked, "Paul, when are you going to stop confusing smarts and popularity with wisdom?" Then he squeezed my shoulder and took off down the stairs. And there I stood.

You have no way of knowing what an impression those words made on me. For days I was angry. I would make a wide circle around Prof Miller when I saw him coming. But slowly his words seeped into my mind and heart, and, finally, I had to admit the good doctor was correct. Even today, they re-enter my consciousness like a caution from the good Lord.

Day 1

Proverbs 4:1–13

1   Hear, ye children, the instruction of a father, and attend to know understanding.

2 For I give you good doctrine, forsake ye not my law.

3 For I was my father's son, tender and only beloved in the sight of my mother.

4 He taught me also, and said unto me, Let thine heart retain my words: keep my commandments, and live.

5 Get wisdom, get understanding: forget it not; neither decline from the words of my mouth.

6 Forsake her not, and she shall preserve thee: love her, and she shall keep thee.

7 Wisdom is the principal thing; therefore get wisdom: and with all thy getting get understanding.

8 Exalt her, and she shall promote thee: she shall bring thee to honour, when thou dost embrace her.

9 She shall give to thine head an ornament of grace: a crown of glory shall she deliver to thee.

10 Hear, O my son, and receive my sayings; and the years of thy life shall be many.

11 I have taught thee in the way of wisdom; I have led thee in right paths.

12 When thou goest, thy steps shall not be straitened; and when thou runnest, thou shalt not stumble.

13 Take fast hold of instruction; let her not go: keep her; for she is thy life.

Reflecting on Proverbs 4:1–13

Meaning, please. . .

ornament of grace (4:9) garland of grace

steps shall not be straitened (4:12) steps shall not be hampered

Read and React

When you peruse these thirteen verses, you discover a different side of King Solomon. He recalls the days in Jerusalem with his father King David and with his mother Bathsheba (1 Chronicles 3:5). Evidently those were happy days for young Solomon. He writes tenderly of both of his parents. He knew that he was "beloved in the sight of his mother."

____ Verses 3-4: There must have been professional teachers in the royal court, but what does Solomon remember of his childhood education? "I was my father's son. . .he taught me also." Parent, understand that your child's education is not limited to a classroom. No teacher is able to provide information about those intangible qualities of life—those that spring from wisdom. That's your responsibility.

____ Verse 4: Solomon recalls, "He taught me, and said to me, 'Let your heart retain my words. Remember to keep the commands I have taught you. And son—you will live!' " Grown child, your Father in heaven is saying the same thing to you through these words.

____ Verses 10–13: "Receive my sayings." While the king asks his son to listen to what he has to say, he also requests that Solomon *receive* his words and ideas. Remember school? Those lessons and lectures when you heard the teacher's words, but you weren't really listening or accepting the words. Perhaps Solomon's eyes glazed over and Father David knew his son wasn't really receiving his words.

Take Inventory

• Listen and read with your mind and heart, as well as with your ears and eyes. Try this poem praising wisdom (3:13–18), that begins and ends with the idea of happiness (using the term "blessed"). As you read these encouraging words, jot down thoughts and reactions that come to mind. Sometimes God speaks to us like this. Be ready to read, digest, and react.

To Memorize

Hear, O my son and receive my sayings; and the years of my life shall be many. Proverbs 4:10

DAY 2

Proverbs 4:14–27

14 Enter not into the path of the wicked, and go not in the way of evil men.

15 Avoid it, pass not by it, turn from it, and pass away.

16 For they sleep not, except they have done mischief; and their sleep is taken away, unless they cause some to fall.

17 For they eat the bread of wickedness, and drink the wine of violence.

18 But the path of the just is as the shining light, that shineth more and more unto the perfect day.

19 The way of the wicked is as darkness: they know not at what they stumble.

20 My son, attend to my words; incline thine ear unto my sayings.

21 Let them not depart from thine eyes; keep them in the midst of thine heart.

22 For they are life unto those that find them, and health to all their flesh.

23 Keep thy heart with all diligence; for out of it are the issues of life.

24 Put away from thee a froward mouth, and perverse lips put far from thee.

25 Let thine eyes look right on, and let thine eyelids look straight before thee.

26 Ponder the path of thy feet, and let all thy ways be established.

27 Turn not to the right hand nor to the left: remove thy foot from evil.

Reflecting on Proverbs 4:14–27

Meaning, please. . .

keep thy heart (4:23) guard your heart

issues of life (4:23) springs of life

a froward mouth (4:24) a deceitful mouth

Read and React

Bread and wine were two of the elements of Israel's everyday life. So Solomon suggests that to those who enter onto the path of the wicked, there will be bread and wine, but they shall be the bread of wickedness and the wine of violence.

Later, in the New Testament, Jesus held in His hands the most common elements of life—bread and wine—to illustrate what was good and necessary. He knew how vital those foods were. They were on the table of the rich and poor alike. They were depended upon for sustenance. They were as common as the twelve men who sat around that table. Today, those elements are at the heart of Christian worship. But Solomon saw them as elements of darkness and death. He selected them to illustrate the commonality of wickedness and violence (4:17). And, according to Solomon, they must be avoided and turned from, else the result is darkness.

____ Verse 14: "Enter not into the path of the wicked." There ought to be an exclamation mark after that statement. Those are strong words. The word *enter* might also be translated, "Don't even step foot onto the path of the wicked." Consider the element of willfulness or volition he implies. No one can use the excuse, "I just found myself skating along that path." Does that speak to you?

____ Verse 15: "Avoid it, pass not by it, turn from it." More exclamation marks needed! Get yourself out of that place!

____ Verse 23: This verse might be expanded and paraphrased, "Your heart is your most precious possession. Guard it with great concern and faithfulness. Don't let it be made foul by those attitudes and actions and words that pervade the path of wickedness."

Take Inventory

As the Solomon poem in this week's introduction observes, all that is good can be "Gone in the wind."

- Where are the promises you have made to yourself and God? Are they gone in the wind?

- Where is the desire to mature in your faith?

- What has happened to your serious pursuit of godly values?

- Pray this prayer: *May the breath of heaven fill my resolve today. May the winds of resolve keep my feet from the path of wickedness. May the Holy Spirit give me direction. Amen.*

To Memorize
Keep thy heart with all diligence; for out of it are the issues of life. Proverbs 4:23

. . .

Day 3

Proverbs 5:1–23

1 My son, attend unto my wisdom, and bow thine ear to my understanding:

2 That thou mayest regard discretion, and that thy lips may keep knowledge.

3 For the lips of a strange woman drop as an honeycomb, and her mouth is smoother than oil:

4 But her end is bitter as wormwood, sharp as a twoedged sword.

5 Her feet go down to death; her steps take hold on hell.

6 Lest thou shouldest ponder the path of life, her ways are moveable, that thou canst not know them.

7 Hear me now therefore, O ye children, and depart not from the words of my mouth.

8 Remove thy way far from her, and come not nigh the door of her house:

9 Lest thou give thine honour unto others, and thy years unto the cruel:

10 Lest strangers be filled with thy wealth; and thy labours be in the house of a stranger;

11 And thou mourn at the last, when thy flesh and thy body are consumed,

12 And say, How have I hated instruction, and my heart despised reproof;

13 And have not obeyed the voice of my teachers, nor inclined mine ear to them that instructed me!

14 I was almost in all evil in the midst of the congregation and assembly.

15 Drink waters out of thine own cistern, and running waters out of thine own well.

16 Let thy fountains be dispersed abroad, and rivers of waters in the streets.

17 Let them be only thine own, and not strangers' with thee.

18 Let thy fountain be blessed: and rejoice with the wife of thy youth.

19 Let her be as the loving hind and pleasant roe; let her breasts satisfy thee at all times; and be thou ravished always with her love.

20 And why wilt thou, my son, be ravished with a strange woman, and embrace the bosom of a stranger?

21 For the ways of man are before the eyes of the LORD, and he pondereth all his goings.

22 His own iniquities shall take the wicked himself, and he shall be holden with the cords of his sins.

23 He shall die without instruction; and in the greatness of his folly he shall go astray.

Reflecting on Proverbs 5:1–23

Meaning, please. . .

attend unto my wisdom (5:1) pay attention. . .

bow thine ear (5:1) listen up!

strange woman (5:3) adulteress

> *her ways are moveable* (5:6) she's on a crooked path, but she doesn't know it
>
> *almost in all evil* (5:14) nearly on the brink of total ruin
>
> *why wilt thou be ravished* (5:20) be captivated

Read and React

Again we enter a discussion of adultery and unchastity. If you feel that Solomon is a bit one-sided in his topics or that he's "beating a dead horse," then open today's newspaper or switch on CNN. As it was in that day, so it is in ours—and maybe more so! The difference? In that day, kings and teachers could call a spade a spade. Issues of morality could be discussed. Those who had gone that way before (like King Solomon) could share what they had learned.

____ Verse 15: After a fourteen-verse description of "giving thine honor to others," the writer suggests, "Drink waters out of thine own cistern, and running waters out of thine own well." To the married person he admonishes the need to get "refreshment" at home. What does this have to say to the unmarried man or woman?

____ Verse 16: Perhaps still smiling, fatherly Solomon continues with some forthright advice: You don't have to share yourself with those who are "abroad"—that is, those who are not under your own roof. Think of the wife of your youth. Solomon must be writing with regret from his own experience, as well as from his father's.

____ Verse 21: Then, as a last resort, Solomon declares, "The ways of man are before the eyes the eyes of the LORD." He sees everything you do.

Take Inventory

• Morally, what is currently "gone in the wind" in your society? In your life? If moral purity is your issue, reread 4;18–27, and then with prayer, "Remove thy foot from evil" (Proverbs 4:27).

The ways of man are before the eyes of the LORD, and he pondereth all his goings. Proverbs 5:21

• • •

Day 4

Proverbs 6:1–19

1 My son, if thou be surety for thy friend, if thou hast stricken thy hand with a stranger,

2 Thou art snared with the words of thy mouth, thou art taken with the words of thy mouth.

3 Do this now, my son, and deliver thyself, when thou art come into the hand of thy friend; go, humble thyself, and make sure thy friend.

4 Give not sleep to thine eyes, nor slumber to thine eyelids.

5 Deliver thyself as a roe from the hand of the hunter, and as a bird from the hand of the fowler.

6 Go to the ant, thou sluggard; consider her ways, and be wise:

7 Which having no guide, overseer, or ruler,

8 Provideth her meat in the summer, and gathereth her food in the harvest.

9 How long wilt thou sleep, O sluggard? when wilt thou arise out of thy sleep?

10 Yet a little sleep, a little slumber, a little folding of the hands to sleep:

11 So shall thy poverty come as one that travelleth, and thy want as an armed man.

12 A naughty person, a wicked man, walketh with a froward mouth.

13 He winketh with his eyes, he speaketh with his feet, he teacheth with his fingers;

14 Frowardness is in his heart, he deviseth mischief continually; he soweth discord.

15 Therefore shall his calamity come suddenly; suddenly shall he be broken without remedy.

16 These six things doth the LORD hate: yea, seven are an abomination unto him:

17 A proud look, a lying tongue, and hands that shed innocent blood,

18 An heart that deviseth wicked imaginations, feet that be swift in running to mischief,

19 A false witness that speaketh lies, and he that soweth discord among brethren.

Reflecting on Proverbs 6:1–19

Meaning, please. . .

if thou be surety (6:1) put up security

stricken thy hand (6:1) shaken hands in a deal

Read and React

In some Bibles, this set of scriptures carries the heading "Dangers of Idleness," in others, it's "Warnings Against Folly," while in a third, it's labeled "Practical Admonitions."

____Verses 6–11: While the foregoing dealt with folly, this passage is definitely a "Practical Admonition." These verses deal with idleness—laziness. And what comes to Solomon's mind to illustrate this truth? He contrasts laziness with the hardworking ant—a household creature well known in the sandy region of Israel.

Solomon realized that immaturity and laziness are a compatible pair. Again, the king's humor shines through verse 10. The words almost sounds like a lullaby lyric with an outrageous punch line—poverty!

Poverty takes many forms besides the lack of money. The lazy student is bereft of education. The lazy fiancé may never have a spouse. The lazy farmer may have more weeds than crops. The lazy soldier may lose his very life.

_____ Verses 16–19: There are seven ugly vices that God hates. Here's the contemporary list: haughty eyes (a proud look), a lying tongue, hands that shed innocent blood, a heart that thinks up wickedness, feet that run to evil, a lying witness, and one who sows discord in a family.

These last four verses should provide grist for plenty of soul searching. There it is in black and white—God hates those seven behavior traits.

Take Inventory

• Reread the seven vices that God hates, listed above, then consider these questions:

• What do proud or haughty eyes reflect?

• What seems to cause a lying tongue?

• Are there other ways of "murdering" a person?

• In our day, does wickedness start in the heart or the mind?

• While this makes it sound as if your feet have a mind of their own, what causes them to go off track?

• What's the difference between a lying tongue and a lying witness?

• How does discord in your family usually start? How do you make peace?

To Memorize

Go to the ant, you sluggard; consider her ways and be wise. Proverbs 6:6

• • •

DAY 5

Proverbs 6:20–35
20 My son, keep thy father's commandment, and forsake not the law of thy mother:

21 Bind them continually upon thine heart, and tie them about thy neck.

22 When thou goest, it shall lead thee; when thou sleepest, it shall keep thee; and when thou awakest, it shall talk with thee.

23 For the commandment is a lamp; and the law is light; and reproofs of instruction are the way of life:

24 To keep thee from the evil woman, from the flattery of the tongue of a strange woman.

25 Lust not after her beauty in thine heart; neither let her take thee with her eyelids.

26 For by means of a whorish woman a man is brought to a piece of bread: and the adulteress will hunt for the precious life.

27 Can a man take fire in his bosom, and his clothes not be burned?

28 Can one go upon hot coals, and his feet not be burned?

29 So he that goeth in to his neighbour's wife; whosoever toucheth her shall not be innocent.

30 Men do not despise a thief, if he steal to satisfy his soul when he is hungry;

31 But if he be found, he shall restore sevenfold; he shall give all the substance of his house.

32 But whoso committeth adultery with a woman lacketh understanding: he that doeth it destroyeth his own soul.

33 A wound and dishonour shall he get; and his reproach shall not be wiped away.

34 For jealousy is the rage of a man: therefore he will not spare in the day of vengeance.

35 He will not regard any ransom; neither will he rest content, though thou givest many gifts.

Reflecting on Proverbs 6:20–35

Meaning, please. . .

goest (6:22) walk

reproofs (6:23) corrections

Read and React

___ Verses 20–21: The Jews bound verses of scripture to their foreheads and hands to serve as reminders of God's commandments. With this in mind, Solomon asks that his son tie the commandments and law to his heart, and to wear them like a necklace. They are to prick the conscience and remind the son of God's expectation for him.

___ Verse 24: "To keep thee from the evil woman, from the flattery of the tongue of a strange woman." How often was the younger Solomon flattered and charmed by the "strange woman"?

Implied throughout this scripture passage is the need of a scripture-sensitive conscience and a realization of the high cost of involvement in sexual sin.

___ Verse 32: What Solomon enumerates above is tragic, but the most tragic loss is the destruction of our very souls.

Take Inventory

• *Loss*—what a bone-chilling word! Our minds reel when we hear it, and we conjure up visions of a desperate mother searching the supermarket aisles, or a knock on the door by a military officer with bad news, or an overwhelming flood of water that sweeps away everything in its way. Loss!

• Remember Jesus' words in the New Testament, "What shall it profit a man, if he shall gain the whole world, and lose his own soul?" (Mark 8:36). Perhaps we can paraphrase that to read, "What will it profit a man or a woman, if he or she has every desire gratified, but in the end loses his or her soul?"

• Spend some time relating that verse and its paraphrase to your desires and needs, both physically and emotionally.

To Memorize
My son, keep thy father's commandment, and forsake not the law of
thy mother. Proverbs 6:20

. . .

Day 6

Proverbs 7:1–23

1 My son, keep my words, And lay up my commandments with thee.

2 Keep my commandments, and live; and my law as the apple of
thine eye.

3 Bind them upon thy fingers, write them upon the table of thine
heart.

4 Say unto wisdom, Thou art my sister; and call understanding thy
kinswoman:

5 That they may keep thee from the strange woman, from the
stranger which flattereth with her words.

6 For at the window of my house I looked through my casement,

7 And beheld among the simple ones, I discerned among the
youths, a young man void of understanding,

8 Passing through the street near her corner; and he went the way
to her house,

9 In the twilight, in the evening, in the black and dark night.

10 And, behold, there met him a woman with the attire of an
harlot, and subtil of heart.

11 (She is loud and stubborn; her feet abide not in her house:

12 Now is she without, now in the streets, and lieth in wait at
every corner.)

13 So she caught him, and kissed him, and with an impudent face
said unto him,

14 I have peace offerings with me; this day have I paid my vows.

15 Therefore came I forth to meet thee, diligently to seek thy face,
and I have found thee.

16 I have decked my bed with coverings of tapestry, with carved

works, with fine linen of Egypt.

17 I have perfumed my bed with myrrh, aloes, and cinnamon.

18 Come, let us take our fill of love until the morning: let us solace ourselves with loves.

19 For the goodman is not at home, he is gone a long journey:

20 He hath taken a bag of money with him, and will come home at the day appointed.

21 With her much fair speech she caused him to yield, with the flattering of her lips she forced him.

22 He goeth after her straightway, as an ox goeth to the slaughter, or as a fool to the correction of the stocks;

23 Till a dart strike through his liver; as a bird hasteneth to the snare, and knoweth not that it is for his life.

Reflecting on Proverbs 7:1–23

Meaning, please. . .

fingers (7:3) hands

peace offerings (7:14) meat used for a religious ceremonial meal

the goodman (7:19) husband

Read and React

These passages hold yet another warning against the adulteress. The focus in this descriptive warning of the "strange woman" is on her enticements.

____ Verses 5, 15: Her flattering words. In today's speech, they might sound like this: "I have selected you, with your handsome face. Now I have found you."

____ Verses 10–11, 13: Her appearance and demeanor. "She was on the street more than at home. She wore the tell-tale clothes of a harlot. She was loud, defiant, impudent, and wouldn't take no for an answer."

_____ Verses 13–20: Her technique. In a word, it's *shrewdness*. She appeals to the young man's inexperience by kissing him and offering him food, followed by tweaking his other senses with perfume and the like. Finally, the woman makes him feel at ease with news that her husband is out of town, and no one will ever know.

It has been said that all forms of temptation involve the same formula for enticement: Make an appeal to the ego, then add the excitement of the senses (consider pornography), followed by the guarantee for ease of acquiring or experiencing.

Has this proven true in your life? Enticement of material possessions, of easy affairs, of credit card spending, of using other people for your own benefit. Wise old Solomon knew nothing of our consumer age, but he realized that his words of wisdom extended beyond the exact situation he presents in Proverbs. Adultery is more than impure people relationships.

Take Inventory
• Reread today's passage from Proverbs. Underline verses or phrases, or single words that speak to you about your kind of temptation. Prayerfully consider your specific temptations in light of Solomon's commands for wisdom.

To Memorize
Keep my commandments, and live. Proverbs 7:2

• • •

Day 7

Proverbs 7:24–27
24 Hearken unto me now therefore, O ye children, and attend to the words of my mouth.
25 Let not thine heart decline to her ways, go not astray in her paths.

26 For she hath cast down many wounded: yea, many strong men have been slain by her.

27 Her house is the way to hell, going down to the chambers of death.

Reflecting on Proverbs 7:24–27

Meaning, please. . .

attend to the words of my mouth (7:24) listen!

heart decline (7:25) heart turn to her ways

cast down many wounded (7:26) victims she brought down

Read and React

> This is the debt I pay
> Just for one riotous day,—
> Years of regret and grief,
> Sorrow without relief.
>
> Pay it I will to the end—
> Until the grave, my friend,
> Gives me a true release,
> Gives me the clasp of peace.
>
> Slight was the thing I bought,
> Small was the debt, I thought,
> Poor was the loan at best—
> God! But the interest.

—PAUL LAWRENCE DUNBAR

Some will classify this bit of verse as old-fashioned and melodramatic as the words of King Solomon. Perhaps so, yet in our more honest moments—perhaps as we read the newspaper or watch television news—we are struck with the similarity of the stories night after night, year after year, and with some changes, century after century.

If we generalize Solomon's tempting harlot into our most contemporary sinful acts and attitudes, we still have a description of how spiritual bankruptcy comes about.

____ Verse 24: Sin centers on each of us when we shut our ears and heart to God's Word.

____ Verse 25: Sin happens when we let our hearts lean toward the ways of the world and our minds to stray over into the world's path.

____ Verse 26: We can be just one of the many victims who are swept away by the tides of unrighteousness.

____ Verse 27: It is a slippery, downward slope, and it leads to death.

So the "strange woman" may or may not be what is keeping you from maturing into the "stature of the fullness of Christ" (Ephesians 4:13). Whatever it is, recognize that life on the dark path demands a payment of deathly interest. Wisdom is the safeguard against adultery.

Take Inventory
• Write a prayer that personalizes 7:24–25. Paraphrase and insert your own straying needs in verse 25. Refer to this prayer often in the days ahead. This is the last session on our adulterous natures.

To Memorize
Let not thine heart decline to her ways, go not astray in her paths. Proverbs 7:25

WEEK THREE
PROVERBS 8 AND 9

If you think political debates get harried, wait until you get into Proverbs 9. Instead of presidential candidates squaring off, it's our lovely Lady Wisdom in this corner, and that sleazy person called Folly in the other corner.

Before we enter chapter 8 and pick up the call to wisdom, we need to consider a bit more the overall influence of Proverbs. There has always been a movement among Christians to remove themselves from the world. Certain orders of sisters went to cloistered convents, where nary a word was spoken, and there was no contact with life outside the convent walls. Earlier there were well-meaning monks who climbed rocky steeps to caves and the like in order to escape the influences of the world. In later years, pious folks took on the plain life, eschewing modern conveniences for the ways of their ancestors in the old country.

Even in recent years, there have been evangelical denominations that have formulated rules of behavior to guarantee their members' holiness and to ensure that all within the fold are of like mind and practice. At one time, education and wisdom were thought of as worldly and would defeat their prescribed way of life, but the numbers within this latter group are diminishing.

Proverbs makes a concentrated effort to lead the Christian community toward the positive influence of human wisdom and experience. Its aim is to offer concrete suggestions on how and how not to go about it. To Solomon, what we call "the real world" includes matters of faith and moral conviction. The proverbs and instructions we find in these thirty-one chapters remind us that we, in the New Testament sense, are part of the world, but not of its mind-set. As we come to the close of this first part of Proverbs, we can almost hear the king telling us that the principles of education, care giving, and business, for instance, are all formed on the basis of moral and religious considerations. To him, it is an absolute given.

A Page from Contemporary Life

When I was a kid in Long Beach, California, Joe Louis was still heavy-weight boxing champion of the world. On fight night, in those pre-television days, we'd sit in front of the tall polished Philco radio, with its green lighted dial and constant hum. This was the same piece of furniture that took me on my *Henry Aldrich* adventure after school, gave mom *Ma Perkins* heartache, and dad (along with all of us) a case of *I Love a Mystery* chills.

None of us were violent people, but the Joe Louis fights were a slice of Americana that dad and I enjoyed together, while mom sat over on the couch and read. We weren't a gambling family, either. But dad and I always had a wager with each other on a Joe Louis fight. We'd bet five cents, and I always got to place my bet on Joe Louis, "The Brown Bomber." Of course, Mr. Louis always won, so dad would walk me down to the Mission Pharmacy for a five-cent ice cream cone.

One time after a fight, on our way to get the ice cream, dad said, "Son, Joe Louis is more than a strong man, he is a wise man, too." I've never forgotten that statement. "The Brown Bomber" had muscles on his muscles, but his heart was as big as the whole outdoors. His kindness was what people outside the ring experienced. Maturity isn't the size of your body, it's the dimension of your heart.

DAY 1

Proverbs 8:1–9

1 Doth not wisdom cry? and understanding put forth her voice?

2 She standeth in the top of high places, by the way in the places of the paths.

3 She crieth at the gates, at the entry of the city, at the coming in at the doors.

4 Unto you, O men, I call; and my voice is to the sons of man.

5 O ye simple, understand wisdom: and, ye fools, be ye of an understanding heart.

6 Hear; for I will speak of excellent things; and the opening of my lips shall be right things.

7 For my mouth shall speak truth; and wickedness is an abomination to my lips.

8 All the words of my mouth are in righteousness; there is nothing froward or perverse in them.

9 They are all plain to him that understandeth, and right to them that find knowledge.

Reflecting on Proverbs 8:1–9

Meaning, please. . .

cry (8:1) call out

places of the paths (8:2) where the paths meet

coming in at the doors (8:3) entrance doors

Read and React

The four days we spend in chapter 8 are like preliminary rounds of a debate, if not a prize fight. In chapter 9, Wisdom and Folly go toe to toe, but here in chapter 8, Wisdom makes a strong case for her value system.

____ Verses 1–4: Lady Wisdom is not some quiet, subtle influence in the world. She knows the importance of her place. Without shame or apology, she accosts all who enter or exit from her presence. Her pronouncements can be heard from mountaintop and valley: "Unto you, O men, I call; and my voice is to the sons of man."

The realization that truth is on our side gives us boldness. Lady Wisdom is about to make a public pronouncement in which she will proclaim her worth (8:6–11), her authority (8:12–16), and her rewards (8:17–21). Again, her boldness is the fruit of divinely given assurance, not limited to the days of Solomon. A wonderful, blind hymn writer named Fanny Crosby declared, "Blessed assurance, Jesus is mine!"

____ Verse 5: The simple and fools come under Wisdom's scrutiny. To the former, she says, " Understand wisdom." Most newer translations read, "Be prudent." The uncomplicated person needs to weigh the value of wisdom. Then he will see that it is God's will that everyone be wise in the things that lead to eternal life.

To the fool, Wisdom advises, "Have an understanding heart." The fool represents those who take no thought for tomorrow, "It'll take care of itself." Such an attitude is a foolish notion, and causes Lady Wisdom to impatiently demand, "Acquire intellegence!"

——— Verses 6–9: After verbally shaking up the simple ones and fools, Lady Wisdom makes another demand, "Listen!" Then she explains why they should listen: "I will speak excellent, truthful, righteous, and just words."

True wisdom fulfills these qualifications, as should the possessor of wisdom: "All the words of my mouth are just, righteous, truthful, and excellent." So, is it possible to possess wisdom to this extent? If it can be promised to the simple and foolish, who are we to be the exceptions?

Take Inventory
Authority and boldness are not negative characteristics, though we

have seen examples of those characteristics that have been a total turnoff. Maturing children of God who seek wisdom will be authentic bearers of these life qualities. Matthew 7:16 says, "Ye shall know them by their fruits."

To Memorize
My mouth shall speak truth. Proverbs 8:7

. . .

DAY 2

Proverbs 8:10–19
10 Receive my instruction, and not silver; and knowledge rather than choice gold.

11 For wisdom is better than rubies; and all the things that may be desired are not to be compared to it.

12 I wisdom dwell with prudence, and find out knowledge of witty inventions.

13 The fear of the LORD is to hate evil: pride, and arrogancy, and the evil way, and the froward mouth, do I hate.

14 Counsel is mine, and sound wisdom: I am understanding; I have strength.

15 By me kings reign, and princes decree justice.

16 By me princes rule, and nobles, even all the judges of the earth.

17 I love them that love me; and those that seek me early shall find me.

18 Riches and honour are with me; yea, durable riches and righteousness.

19 My fruit is better than gold, yea, than fine gold; and my revenue than choice silver.

Reflecting on Proverbs 8:10–19

Meaning, please. . .

witty inventions (8:12) I possess knowledge and discretion

counsel (8:14) godly advice

durable riches and righteousness (8:18)
enduring wealth and prosperity

my revenue (8:19) what I yield

Read and React

Within the ten verses of this selection, Lady Wisdom continues to build a case for her ability to outperform Folly. Here she enumerates reasons for her superiority. While you read through this list, ask yourself how far Solomon expects us mere mortals to go to incorporate these absolutes into our minds and hearts.

____ Verse 10: Turn down riches for wisdom. Who among us are given that opportunity? Still, there have been Christian leaders who, earlier in their lives, turned down influential and well-paying careers in order to do God's will. Not everyone is asked to do this, but the maturing Christian is ready to do so if asked.

____ Verse 11: Wisdom is not only better than gold and silver, it's better than possessing rubies. According to Lady Wisdom, nothing you could ever want or ask for equals the value of wisdom.

____ Verse 13: To be a God-honoring believer, it is necessary to hate evil—pride, arrogance, evil behavior, and perverse speech.

At this point Lady Wisdom appears to turn a corner in her pronouncement, and she looks more intimately at what characterizes the Lord and what He is able to do.

____ Verse 14: Wise counsel is what He offers. How does He counsel you?

___ Verse 14: He has great strength. Do you take advantage of His strength?

___ Verses 15–16: Because He gives wisdom, strength, and understanding, great leaders are able to reign. Are there contemporary examples of world leaders who depend upon the Lord?

___ Verse 17: Because He loves you, you feel His drawing, causing you to seek Him and surrender to His will.

Finally, He spells out the temporal rewards of those who follow Him.

___ Verse 18: He reminds you that the riches of His resources stand behind His promise of righteousness. Because He loves you, you shall share in His riches.

___ Verse 19: With all the talk of gold and jewels and other treasures, He is aware that your greatest need is the Spirit. His fruit (eternal life) is the finest gift He can give you.

Tomorrow's lesson begins where this closes.

Take Inventory

• Has the Lord spoken to you through this scripture passage? These first eight chapters of Proverbs provide strong spiritual direction. Today's study becomes very personal. It is a reminder of what the Lord has to offer: strength, wisdom, understanding, love, righteousness, and eternal life.

• Spend a few minutes in conversation with the Father. Ask Him if you have fully accepted all that He offers.

To Memorize

Those that seek me early shall find me. Proverbs 8:17

Day 3

Proverbs 8:20–31

20 I lead in the way of righteousness, in the midst of the paths of judgment:

21 That I may cause those that love me to inherit substance; and I will fill their treasures.

22 The LORD possessed me in the beginning of his way, before his works of old.

23 I was set up from everlasting, from the beginning, or ever the earth was.

24 When there were no depths, I was brought forth; when there were no fountains abounding with water.

25 Before the mountains were settled, before the hills was I brought forth:

26 While as yet he had not made the earth, nor the fields, nor the highest part of the dust of the world.

27 When he prepared the heavens, I was there: when he set a compass upon the face of the depth:

28 When he established the clouds above: when he strengthened the fountains of the deep:

29 When he gave to the sea his decree, that the waters should not pass his commandment: when he appointed the foundations of the earth:

30 Then I was by him, as one brought up with him: and I was daily his delight, rejoicing always before him;

31 Rejoicing in the habitable part of his earth; and my delights were with the sons of men.

Reflecting on Proverbs 8:20–31

Meaning, please. . .

inherit substance (8:21) bestowing wealth

no depths (8:24) no oceans

as one brought up with him (8:30) as a master worker

Read and React

Still preparing for chapter 9 and her "contest" with Folly, Lady Wisdom continues to present her "resume." Her credentials are impeccable. After all, she has been around as long as the Father Himself. On the other hand, Folly is as old as the Garden of Eden, if not older.

___ Verses 20–21: Wisdom reminds us that she has walked the path of righteousness and justice since the beginning of time.

Need proof of the presence of wisdom since the beginning? Look around you; there had to be wise planning in the creation of our world and its universe!

> *This is a piece too fair*
> *To be the child of Chance, and not of Care.*
> *No Atoms casually together hurl'd*
> *Could e'er produce so beautiful a world.*

> —JOHN DRYDEN

___ Verses 22–29: Lady Wisdom continues to build upon her premise that she was with the Father since the beginning. She describes her divine origin (8:22, 24, 26) before anything else was created, and she asserts this throughout the full passage.

___ Verses 30–31: She was at God's side as a "master worker." A right hand, as it were, in the creation process. According to her testimony, she was daily His delight, and she took delight in His creation of the whole world, including mankind.

From other lyrics by John Dryden, "O to have been there when the morning stars sang together; When the Creator, in His great Wisdom, breathed His spirit into man."

Take Inventory

- "I was daily his delight," (8:30) says Lady Wisdom. Even this "grand lady" realizes the importance of delighting the Father. At the end of this day, pray about delighting Him. And where is your delight?

To Memorize

I was daily his delight, rejoicing always before him. Proverbs 8:30

. . .

DAY 4

Proverbs 8:32–36

32 Now therefore hearken unto me, O ye children: for blessed are they that keep my ways.

33 Hear instruction, and be wise, and refuse it not.

34 Blessed is the man that heareth me, watching daily at my gates, waiting at the posts of my doors.

35 For whoso findeth me findeth life, and shall obtain favour of the LORD.

36 But he that sinneth against me wrongeth his own soul: all they that hate me love death.

Reflecting on Proverbs 8:32–36

Meaning, please. . .

blessed (8:32) held in reverence, honored

favour (8:35) friendly regard shown toward another

Read and React

Lady Wisdom's qualifications have been given for all to hear. Perhaps the most notable being the fact that she was with our Creator from the very beginning. Standing somewhere in a shadow is Dame Folly, awaiting her turn to impress you.

___ Verses 32–33: An original contemporary rendition: "So now that you have heard my qualifications, listen up! I have every right to instruct you. If you heed my instructions and follow them, you will be blessed. If you don't, well. . ."

Who doesn't want to be blessed? Take another look at what being blessed entails; pleasure, contentment, good fortune. How unwise to turn your back on that kind of a deal. This particular blessing is the gift of wisdom.

___ Verse 34: Lady Wisdom focuses in on one particular recipient of the Father's blessing. It is one of the persons who listened to her wise counsel. He's the one who is so eager to receive wisdom that he sits and waits outside her door.

___ Verses 35–36: Finally Lady Wisdom gets to the bottom line: "Whoso findeth me findeth life." Stripping away all the King James grammar, she is telling you, "When you look for and find God, you find *life!*" And in finding life, you are in God's favor.

Unfortunately, there is an opposite truth here, too. If verse 35 is true, then there must be a verse 36. Sinning against the Father results in death. "They that hate me and my way, love death." Hate is an unusually strong word. Why would anyone in his or her right mind *hate* God?

"He who fails to find me," says the Father, "kills himself." That certainly tells you who's responsible for your eternal life, doesn't it? It's not a vindictive God who condemns you to death—you do it yourself!

Take Inventory

• Have you ever considered writing a short, spiritual autobiography? In light of what we have just read through together, find a quiet place, a notebook or piece of paper, and explain on paper how verses 35 and 36 relate to you. Prayerfully think about how you found God, or hope to find God. If you feel comfortable doing it, share your spiritual autobiography with someone else.

To Memorize

For whoso findeth me findeth life. Proverbs 8:35

. . .

DAY 5

Proverbs 9:1–6

1 Wisdom hath builded her house, she hath hewn out her seven pillars:

2 She hath killed her beasts; she hath mingled her wine; she hath also furnished her table.

3 She hath sent forth her maidens: she crieth upon the highest places of the city,

4 Whoso is simple, let him turn in hither: as for him that wanteth understanding, she saith to him,

5 Come, eat of my bread, and drink of the wine which I have mingled.

6 Forsake the foolish, and live; and go in the way of understanding.

Reflecting on Proverbs 9:1–6

Meaning, please. . .

killed her beasts (9:2) prepared her meat

> *mingled wine* (9:2) wine mixed with spices
>
> *turn in hither* (9:4) turn in here
>
> *the foolish* (9:6) the immature

Read and React

Lady Wisdom offers her invitation to a banquet, where we know at least bread, meat, and mixed wine will be served. Her guest list is made up of the immature and unwise—the simple. Her serving girls are ready. She goes to a high place where she directs traffic. "Turn in here," she calls out to passersby.

At the same time, Dame Folly is preparing her refreshments. She plans to lure in the simple with a drink of stolen water, that she calls sweet (9:17).

____ Verses 1–3: In chapter 9, the scene changes to a realistic setting. We discover Lady Wisdom in her home preparing a banquet. Her table is lovingly set with her finest tableware. The bread has been taken from the oven; the best wine is mulled and mixed with pungent spices; the young women who will serve are standing by.

____ Verses 4–6: As if the aroma of her meal isn't enough of a lure, Lady Wisdom goes out where the people are passing. "Want a delicious meal? Come in and eat my home-cooked meal." Needless to say, this was written before church suppers, but the motivation should the be same! In a post–New Testament way of doing things, wisdom and evangelism drive God's children out into the highways and byways to compel others in.

Wisdom's message to those who stream by? "Put aside your immaturity, and find genuine life!" Then, "Walk in the path of understanding" to grow in your experience with God.

Take Inventory

• In the privacy of your quiet time, think about wisdom. Who in your family or acquaintances has the characteristics that make you feel he or she is wise?

To Memorize
Forsake the foolish, and live; and go in the way of understanding.
Proverbs 9:6

• • •

Day 6

Proverbs 9:7–12
7 He that reproveth a scorner getteth to himself shame: and he that rebuketh a wicked man getteth himself a blot.

8 Reprove not a scorner, lest he hate thee: rebuke a wise man, and he will love thee.

9 Give instruction to a wise man, and he will be yet wiser: teach a just man, and he will increase in learning.

10 The fear of the LORD is the beginning of wisdom: and the knowledge of the holy is understanding.

11 For by me thy days shall be multiplied, and the years of thy life shall be increased.

12 If thou be wise, thou shalt be wise for thyself: but if thou scornest, thou alone shalt bear it.

Reflecting on Proverbs 9:7–12

Meaning, please. . .

a blot (9:7) a hurt

reprove (9:7, 8) correct

scorner (9:8) scoffer

Read and React

While Dame Folly prepares her party to lure the simpleminded onto the dark path that leads to hell, Lady Wisdom continues to share various parables and aphorisms on wisdom.

_____ Verses 7–8: It seems that Wisdom admits that there are scoffers with whom it is often difficult to share the Good News. There are times, when in your attempt to bring God's love to the attention of those who scorn, there's a good chance you'll end up with a wounded nose.

But it's a different story when you rebuke a wise man; he will love you for your concern.

When you instruct a wise man, he understands that he will be wiser for it. Such a just man will increase his learning.

_____ Verse 10: Perhaps all that has preceded this verse has been a preamble to the truth of these ten words: "The fear of the LORD is the beginning of wisdom." Don't stumble over the word *fear*. It is a righteous word, in spite of the synonyms in *Roget's Thesaurus*: fear, dread, fright, alarm, panic, terror, trepidation. But in very small type, Webster says, "Profound reverence and awe, especially toward God."

Such a love and respect for God produces wisdom. While learning about God will often generate an emotion of respect, Lady Wisdom wants us to know that a deep understanding of who God is and what He has done for His people will bring about heart wisdom.

_____ Verse 11: Such a positive relationship with God is not all one-sided. As a Father, He knows how to treat His children. Your days will be multiplied and your years increased.

Now, face it, there may be days that you don't want multiplied. But, think about it—if you're in a tight relationship with your heavenly Father, days may take on a new luster.

It's amazing how special days become more special when you're in sync with the Father. Remember as a kid when you were in the middle of doing something so much fun that you wished the day would never end? To sons and daughters of the Father, even lousy days are better because He is present.

___ Verse 12: Then Lady Wisdom zaps us with, "If you are wise, you will be rewarded by your own wisdom; but if you scoff at the things of God, only you will suffer." This is Wisdom's stress on personal responsibility.

Take Inventory

• Proverbs emphasizes need for personal responsibility. A quote from William J. Bennett is appropriate here: "Responsible persons are mature people who have taken charge of themselves and their conduct, who own their actions and own up to them."

• And Jesus said, "For unto whomsoever much is given, of him shall be much required" (Luke 12:48).

• And you say. . .

To Memorize

The fear of the LORD is the beginning of wisdom. Proverbs 9:10

. . .

DAY 7

Proverbs 9:13–18

13 A foolish woman is clamorous: she is simple, and knoweth nothing.

14 For she sitteth at the door of her house, on a seat in the high places of the city,

15 To call passengers who go right on their ways:

16 Whoso is simple, let him turn in hither: and as for him that wanteth understanding, she saith to him,

17 Stolen waters are sweet, and bread eaten in secret is pleasant.

18 But he knoweth not that the dead are there; and that her guests are in the depths of hell.

Reflecting on Proverbs 9:13–18

Meaning, please. . .

clamorous (9:13) loud

passengers (9:15) those who pass by

Read and React

Well, this is it. This is where Dame Folly makes herself known. You'll recall that this passage and the first of this chapter run simultaneously. While Lady Wisdom was cooking and setting her table, in another part of town Ms. Folly was preparing her trap for the unsuspecting.

____ Verse 13: This is *so* Dame Foolish. Solomon describes her as being clamorous. Maybe he was trying to be nice and keep from calling her loud, or "noisily insistent," but that's her all over!

____ Verses 14–16: Yes, she may "knoweth nothing," but she certainly knew that she was going to be in competition with Lady Wisdom for the hearts of the simple folk. That's why she sat at her door and motioned for the simple to come into her driveway and up on her porch.

____ Verse 18: Too bad, but those simple folks may have driven right past Lady Wisdom's front door with all the blessings she had to offer and found themselves in Dame Folly's driveway. Little did they know that the dead were there, and at that very moment, they were in the depths of hell.

Quite a dramatic closing. There are times when we wonder what the ratio of Dame Folly's guests, to those who stopped by Lady Wisdom's place. Can it be spelled out any plainer? We have a choice to make—heaven or hell!

Take Inventory

- Dame Folly is indeed a character. She could just as well be christened Sir Folly, but Solomon gave both Wisdom and Folly the female gender. Folly, foolishness, and fool are all cut from the same pattern— they are one. Perhaps everyone has a bit of folly in him or her, and it must be faced and prayed over.

To Memorize

Whom the LORD loveth he correcteth; even as a father the son in whom he delighteth. Proverbs 3:12

WEEK FOUR

Now begins a collection of unrelated, individual proverbial sayings, fittingly titled "The Proverbs of Solomon." These extend to Proverbs 22:16. They really have no continuity or pattern but are a large number of proverbs selected from Solomon's vast collection.

Here is a bit of trivia, in case you ever need it for a game or a lagging conversation: According to a Bible sourcebook, the numerical values of the consonants in the Hebrew word for Solomon total 375, the exact number of verses in 10:1 to 22:16. To the Hebrew mind, this was significant. It is something akin to Psalm 119, where each stanza begins with the letters of the Hebrew alphabet.

This new section of the book, "The Proverbs of Solomon," presents his wise sayings in a narrower sense, nearer to what we expect them to be. They can be divided into four general categories:

1. Observations about how life is (e.g., 10:4, 12, 26)
2. Observations about wisdom (e.g., 10:1, 5, 8)
3. Observations about righteousness (e.g., 10:2, 6–7)
4. Observations about God's involvement in people's lives (e.g., 10:3, 22, 27)

A Page from Contemporary Life

"Dad, why are we so poor?" nine-year-old Lisa blurted out at dinner one evening.

"Why do you ask?" I inquired, glancing at her mother, who lowered her eyes and made herself busy with a tomato slice.

"Well, Jenny's dad is taking her and the whole family skiing at Whistler for Christmas."

"Let's talk about it after dinner," I answered, knowing full well Lisa had to have an answer right then.

"Dad!" was her response.

"After dinner!" was mine.

I knew Jenny's dad was a big spender. I also knew that he lived beyond his means and that he was delinquent in his payments to the company I worked for and half the other subcontractors in town. He was about to file Chapter Thirteen. When I'd see that television commercial about the guy in debt up to his eyeballs, I'd think of Jenny's dad.

Sure enough, when we pushed back from the diner table, Lisa announced, "Okay, now we're gonna talk!" So talk we did, while Mom filled the dishwasher.

"Honey, first of all, we are not poor. God has been good to our family. I can make the mortgage payment on the house and pay the utility and other bills as they come in."

"Doesn't Jenny's dad do that, too?" Lisa interrupted.

"We're not talking about him."

"Sorry."

"Your mom and I give to the church, too, Lisa."

"But what has that to do with a ski trip over Christmas?"

"Plenty, honey. Because we are thankful for our good health, my job, and the other things God helps us with, we give to our church and its work."

"Jenny and her folks don't go to church," Lisa responded.

I wanted to say, "Yeah, and her dad doesn't pay his bills either." But I didn't. Instead I told my daughter, "By the time we pay all the bills; give our church pledge; shell out for lunch monies, Friday nights at Wendy's, and an occasional movie; *and* put some away in savings, there isn't much left for an exotic ski trip to Whistler."

That night, Lisa's Bible storybook had a verse from Proverbs: "The blessing of the LORD makes one rich, and He adds no sorrow with it" (10:22 NKJV).

Day 1

Proverbs 10:1–8

1 The Proverbs of Solomon. A wise son maketh a glad father: but a foolish son is the heaviness of his mother.

2 Treasures of wickedness profit nothing: but righteousness delivereth from death.

3 The Lord will not suffer the soul of the righteous to famish: but he casteth away the substance of the wicked.

4 He becometh poor that dealeth with a slack hand: but the hand of the diligent maketh rich.

5 He that gathereth in summer is a wise son: but he that sleepeth in harvest is a son that causeth shame.

6 Blessings are upon the head of the just: but violence covereth the mouth of the wicked.

7 The memory of the just is blessed: but the name of the wicked shall rot.

8 The wise in heart will receive commandments: but a prating fool shall fall.

Reflecting on Proverbs 10:1–8

Meaning, please. . .

suffer (10:3) allow

slack (10:4) lazy

prating (10:8) jabbering

Read and React

Today's lesson has much to say about laziness—certainly a hindrance to massing wealth.

___ Verse 1: Serving as a preface to the rest of the chapter, this first verse recaps the spirit of what has gone before. Mother and father are still recipients of their son's behavior, be it wise or foolish. Can't you imagine the mother of this son, after he's done something really foolish, saying with a sigh, "Such is a mother's lot." Is Solomon trying to tell us that fathers bond with wise sons, while sons who are foolish turn to their mothers?

___Verse 2: Old Testament history indicates that an early or unsavory death is punishment for sin, while long life is the reward for the wise and righteous. Today, medical science can vouch for the toll that debauched living takes on the human body. I'm not sure Solomon has a pithy saying to cover when bad things happen to good people. Verse 2 continues the same thought.

___Verses 4–5: Slack hands and those who sleep through harvest are the less desirable workers on this farm. As a matter of fact, the farmer who has a slacker on his crew will become poor, while on the other hand, the farm hand who is wise will make his boss rich. There is no mention of how the farm hand himself will fare.

It is important that those who study the Bible, both Old and New Testaments, remember that this was a rural, agrarian society. How is this message appropriate to your line of work? How does laziness show itself today?

___ Verses 6–8: Here is another group of contrasts featuring the wise and the just versus the wicked and jabbering fool. Who are the just? The meaning of the word? It is the root for these familiar biblical words: justification, justice, justify.

A key Old Testament "justice" verse: "What doth the LORD require of thee, but to do justly, and to love mercy, and to walk humbly with thy God?" (Micah 6:8).

Here are key New Testament references to investigate: 2 Thessalonians 1:6; 1 John 1:9; Revelation 15:3; Matthew 12:18; Acts 13:39; Romans 3:24, 4:25, 5:1, 8:30; Titus 3:7.

Take Inventory

- Consider what it means to be just. A dictionary definition is "being in conformity to what is morally fair, upright or good." How does the Micah 6:8 relate to Solomon's use of *just*? In what way can you or do you exercise justice?

To Memorize

While not from Proverbs, this is a scripture verse that needs to be memorized and put into use every day:

What doth the LORD require of thee, but to do justly, and to love mercy, and to walk humbly with thy God? Micah 6:8

• • •

DAY 2

Proverbs 10:9–23

9 He that walketh uprightly walketh surely: but he that perverteth his ways shall be known.

10 He that winketh with the eye causeth sorrow: but a prating fool shall fall.

11 The mouth of a righteous man is a well of life: but violence covereth the mouth of the wicked. But love covereth all sins.

12 Hatred stirreth up strifes: but love covereth all sins.

13 In the lips of him that hath understanding wisdom is found: but a rod is for the back of him that is void of understanding.

14 Wise men lay up knowledge: but the mouth of the foolish is near destruction.

15 The rich man's wealth is his strong city: the destruction of the poor is their poverty.

16 The labor of the righteous tendeth to life: the fruit of the wicked to sin.

17 He is in the way of life that keepeth instruction: but he that refuseth reproof erreth.

18 He that hideth hatred with lying lips, and he that uttereth a slander, is a fool.

19 In the multitude of words there wanteth not sin: but he that refraineth his lips is wise.

20 The tongue of the just is as choice silver: the heart of the wicked is little worth.

21 The lips of the righteous feed many: but fools die for want of wisdom.

22 The blessing of the LORD, it maketh rich, and he addeth no sorrow with it.

23 It is as sport to a fool to do mischief: but a man of understanding hath wisdom.

Reflecting on Proverbs 10:9–23

Meaning, please. . .

uprightly (10:9) with integrity

shall be known (10:9) shall be found out

winketh (10:10) the gesture of a lewd person

prating (10:10) jabbering

well (10:11) fountain

strong city (10:15) fortified city

labor (10:16) wages

Read and React

These words in chapter 10 and the following may appear to be a haphazard collection of aphorisms and sayings. But if read in their original language, the reader would discover catchwords, plays on words, alliteration, and words and phrases that sound alike, which give more reason for their order and inclusion.

At this point, Lady Wisdom and Dame Folly are in the wings while we play out on the stage of life our acceptance or rejection of their instruction. The thirteen proverbs in this passage highlight some of our most soul-damning behavior and words, as well as the possibility for our righteous moments. Which shall it be?

Soul-Damning Behavior		Results
Perverted life	10:9	Will be found out
Winks maliciously	10:10	Cause sorrow
Jabbering fool	10:10	Will fall
Violence	10:11	A wicked mouth
Hatred	10:12	Stirs up strife
Void of understanding	10:13	A rod on the back
Mouth of foolishness	10:14	Near destruction
Destruction of poor	10:15	Their poverty
Sin	10:16	Fruit of the wicked
Refuses correction	10:17	Error

Righteous Behavior		Results
Walk uprightly	10:9	Walk with assurance
Righteous mouth	10:11	A well of life
Love	10:12	Covers all sins
Understanding lips	10:13	Wisdom is found
Lay up knowledge	10:14	Wisdom
Rich man's wealth	10:15	His fortress
Labor of the Righteous	10:16	Brings the life
Keeps instruction	10:17	In the way of life

Throughout this listing of illicit behavior and righteous behavior, there is a presupposition, "the fear of the Lord is the beginning of wisdom."

Take Inventory

• Take the above lists seriously. In a quiet moment, try your hand at paraphrasing them to fit your own life. The Bible is surely the Word of God. While other literature may be written in high-sounding prose, it does not have the power to change a person's spirit and soul. If you're not doing it now, begin having a daily quiet time with God. Find a Bible version that suits you, then spend time in it, along with prayer.

To Memorize
The tongue of the just is as choice silver. Proverbs 10:20

. . .

Day 3

Proverbs 10:24–32
24 The fear of the wicked, it shall come upon him: but the desire of the righteous shall be granted.

25 As the whirlwind passeth, so is the wicked no more: but the righteous is an everlasting foundation.

26 As vinegar to the teeth, and as smoke to the eyes, so is the sluggard to them that send him.

27 The fear of the LORD prolongeth days: but the years of the wicked shall be shortened.

28 The hope of the righteous shall be gladness: but the expectation of the wicked shall perish.

29 The way of the LORD is strength to the upright: but destruction shall be to the workers of iniquity.

30 The righteous shall never be removed: but the wicked shall not inhabit the earth.

31 The mouth of the just bringeth forth wisdom: but the froward tongue shall be cut out.

32 The lips of the righteous know what is acceptable: but the mouth of the wicked speaketh frowardness.

Reflecting on Proverbs 10:24–32

Meaning, please. . .

fear of the wicked (10:24) what the wicked dread
whirlwind (10:25) tempest
an everlasting foundation (10:25) established forever
them that send (10:26) employers
froward (10:31) perverse

Read and React

This is a continuation of proverbial contrasts between the righteous and the wicked. By this time, we have a good understanding what a proverb is. For those of us who are still wondering, the following are explanations of the character of a parable. Read them with an eye to Solomon's Proverbs.

"A proverb is a short sentence based on long experience" (Cervantes).

"A frequent review of parables, especially those of Solomon, should enter into our reading" (Disraeli).

"A proverb is no proverb till your life has illustrated it" (Keats).

"Solomon made a book of proverbs, a book of proverbs never made a Solomon" (an English saying).

Nor does reading a book of proverbs make us righteous or wicked. Both heart conditions are considered at length in this passage.

Righteousness. In chapters 10–13 the word *righteous(ness)* occurs twenty-one times, as does the word *wicked(ness)*. That may be something of a record in scripture but not surprising in these verses of contrast.

The nature of righteousness is described as "straight," "correct," "orderly," "proper," and "most fair." In Proverbs, it is closely related to "uprightness," which is better translated from the original Hebrew as "straightness," which is closely related to "integrity" and "wholeness." Some modern translators have selected "blameless" as a synonym. Though out Proverbs, righteousness reveals itself as "honesty," "sympathy," "justice," and "truth."

Wickedness. In contrast to righteousness, wickedness represents what is untrue and out of sync. It can take the form of "crookedness." Some contemporary versions of Proverbs have selected the words "perverse," "rebellious," "crooked," and "sin."

Wickedness often suggests going astray from the right path. It can be found in craftiness and devising evil. It expresses itself in dishonesty, deceitfulness, and "getting even."

___ Verse 26: "As vinegar to the teeth, and as smoke to the eyes, so is the sluggard to them that send him." Solomon never has a good thing to say about the lazy. While only accusing them of being an irritation, like vinegar and smoke, he implies that they aren't worthy of consideration. With a verbal gesture he passes them off.

___ Verse 28: "Hope" and "expectation" are the key words in this verse of contrast. The righteous have hope, but the expectation of the wicked will perish. Is there a difference between "hope" and "expectation"?

Take Inventory
• In the spirit of Solomon, make a list of your hopes and your expectations. Reflect on how one is more "spiritual" than the other. Or is that true? Was Solomon just using a synonym? Is the author not making a value judgment on "expectation"?

To Memorize
The fear of the LORD prolongeth days. Proverbs 10:27

Day 4

Proverbs 11:1–15

1 A false balance is abomination to the LORD: but a just weight is his delight.

2 When pride cometh, then cometh shame: but with the lowly is wisdom.

3 The integrity of the upright shall guide them: but the perverseness of transgressors shall destroy them.

4 Riches profit not in the day of wrath: but righteousness delivereth from death.

5 The righteousness of the perfect shall direct his way: but the wicked shall fall by his own wickedness.

6 The righteousness of the upright shall deliver them: but transgressors shall be taken in their own naughtiness.

7 When a wicked man dieth, his expectation shall perish: and the hope of unjust men perisheth.

8 The righteous is delivered out of trouble, and the wicked cometh in his stead.

9 A hypocrite with his mouth destroyeth his neighbour: but through knowledge shall the just be delivered.

10 When it goeth well with the righteous, the city rejoiceth: and when the wicked perish, there is shouting.

11 By the blessing of the upright the city is exalted: but it is overthrown by the mouth of the wicked.

12 He that is void of wisdom despiseth his neighbour: but a man of understanding holdeth his peace.

13 A talebearer revealeth secrets: but he that is of a faithful spirit concealeth the matter.

14 Where no counsel is, the people fall: but in the multitude of counsellors there is safety.

15 He that is surety for a stranger shall smart for it: and he that hateth suretiship is sure.

Reflecting on Proverbs 11:1–15

Meaning, please. . .

balance, weight (11:1) a reference to scales

perfect (11:5) upright, spiritually mature, blameless

shouting (11:10) jubilation

surety for a stranger (11:15) to guarantee a loan

Read and React

We continue Proverbs with its seeming hit-or-miss collection of sayings. Throughout these thirty-one chapters, there are countless soul- and mind-jarring hits, and few, if any, misses. There's good reasoning behind this fact, even though it seems to be a grab bag of sayings from many sources. God has kept His hand on this anthology of righteousness.

___ Verse 1: The issue of cheating leads off chapter 11. While weigh scales mean little to us today, many of a certain age will remember a Norman Rockwell cover on *The Saturday Evening Post* in which a butcher is weighing a steak. Unbeknownst to the customer, the butcher has left his thumb on the scale. And unbeknownst to the butcher, the sweet little lady is pushing up on the bottom of the scale with her thumb.

In Deuteronomy 25:13–15 it is written, "Thou shalt not have in thy bag divers different weights, a great and a small. Thou shalt not have in thine house divers measures, a great and a small. But thou shalt have a perfect and just weight, a perfect and just measure shalt thou have; that thy days may be lengthened."

To many, cheating has almost become second nature. Is cheating always stealing? A quick answer—yes! Whether you are a student who uses crib notes for an exam, or you park in a handicap zone, or you smuggle an overdue library book back on the shelf. It's all benefiting yourself, at the expense of someone else.

Take Inventory

• The focus of today's study has been on the first verse of chapter 11. Read all 15 verses and make personal discoveries for yourself. The topics are as varied as hypocrisy (11:9), gossip (11:13), and security (11:15).

To Memorize

A man of understanding holdeth his peace. Proverbs 11:12

• • •

Day 5

Proverbs 11:16–31

16 A gracious woman retaineth honour: and strong men retain riches.

17 The merciful man doeth good to his own soul: but he that is cruel troubleth his own flesh.

18 The wicked worketh a deceitful work: but to him that soweth righteousness shall be a sure reward.

19 As righteousness tendeth to life; so he that pursueth evil pursueth it to his own death.

20 They that are of a froward heart are abomination to the LORD: but such as are upright in their way are his delight.

21 Though hand join in hand, the wicked shall not be unpunished: but the seed of the righteous shall be delivered.

22 As a jewel of gold in a swine's snout, so is a fair woman which is without discretion.

23 The desire of the righteous is only good: but the expectation of the wicked is wrath.

24 There is that scattereth, and yet increaseth; and there is that withholdeth more than is meet, but it tendeth to poverty.

25 The liberal soul shall be made fat: and he that watereth shall be watered also himself.

26 He that withholdeth corn, the people shall curse him: but blessing shall be upon the head of him that selleth it.

27 He that diligently seeketh good procureth favour: but he that seeketh mischief, it shall come unto him.

28 He that trusteth in his riches shall fall: but the righteous shall flourish as a branch.

29 He that troubleth his own house shall inherit the wind: and the fool shall be servant to the wise of heart.

30 The fruit of the righteous is a tree of life; and he that winneth souls is wise.

31 Behold, the righteous shall be recompensed in the earth: much more the wicked and the sinner.

Reflecting on Proverbs 11:16–31

Meaning, please. . .

hand join in hand (11:21) be assured

Read and React

Solomon is no respecter of genders. While the males have been painted as lazy louts, adulterers, liars, and cheaters, a female has been presented to us as the paragon of wisdom. By the same token, Dame Folly deservedly earned a negative reputation. In this study passage, the proverb collectors found more description of womanhood.

___ Verse 16: A gracious woman retains honor. The word *gracious* is a highly complimentary description of a woman in any situation. Some modern English versions of this scripture have selected the descriptive word *kindhearted.* Can you imagine what kindheartedness accomplished in those BC days? One female minister recently said, "For a woman to be gracious in a day when females were sold like so much chattel, it was obvious that God was at work within her."

___ Verse 24: There is a stewardship lesson here. A free paraphrase: "There are those who give to the Lord's work freely, even without a large back account. This might be called proportioned giving.

But it is presented with a glad heart. And the miracle is, God blesses them, and their earnings increase. Others grunt and groan about giving, and the result is, they suffer want, both in their bank accounts and in their spirits."

___ Verse 30: The tree of life, what a good picture. If you are a visual person, you might see what this writer sees: a tall leafy tree with juicy pears hanging all over it. When you walk over to it and reach up and pick a piece of fruit, you discover that there is the photo of a person's face on every one of those pears. They are the fruit of your righteousness. They are the individuals who have come across your path, and who were influenced by your testimony or kindness.

Take Inventory
• The fruit of your righteousness. Are there any "pears" in your life? Ask the Lord to impress you with the name or face of a person who could use your kindness, your caring, your encouragement, your good word for the Lord.

To Memorize
The desire of the righteous is only good. Proverbs 11:23

· · ·

DAY 6

Proverbs 12:1–13
1 Whoso loveth instruction loveth knowledge: but he that hateth reproof is brutish.

2 A good man obtaineth favor of the LORD: but a man of wicked devices will he condemn.

3 A man shall not be established by wickedness: but the root of the righteous shall not be moved.

4 A virtuous woman is a crown to her husband: but she that maketh ashamed is as rottenness in his bones.

5 The thoughts of the righteous are right: but the counsels of the wicked are deceit.

6 The words of the wicked are to lie in wait for blood: but the mouth of the upright shall deliver them.

7 The wicked are overthrown, and are not: but the house of the righteous shall stand.

8 A man shall be commended according to his wisdom: but he that is of a perverse heart shall be despised.

9 He that is despised, and hath a servant, is better than he that honoreth himself, and lacketh bread.

10 A righteous man regardeth the life of his beast: but the tender mercies of the wicked are cruel.

11 He that tilleth his land shall be satisfied with bread: but he that followeth vain persons is void of understanding.

12 The wicked desireth the net of evil men: but the root of the righteous yieldeth fruit.

13 The wicked is snared by the transgression of his lips: but the just shall come out of trouble.

Reflecting on Proverbs 12:1–13

Meaning, please. . .

reproof (12:1) correction

instruction (12:1) discipline

virtuous (12:4) of noble character

maketh ashamed (12:4) brings shame

followeth vain persons (12:11) chases fantasies

net (12:12) plunder

Read and React

Much comment is made over the differences between the God of the Old Testament and the God of the New Testament. There is another contrast between the Old and New Testaments—the role of women in that society. Our study of Proverbs seems to bear this out to a point. Granted, the "men" referred to in these parables is often generic "man," meaning what goes for one gender goes for the other.

Women in the New Testament, while bound by ancient codes of behavior, are generally introduced with a tenderness—a quality missing in much of the Old Testament. Notable exceptions are Ruth, Esther, Miriam, et al. Most critics believe that the New Testament view of women is a direct result of Jesus and His teachings. Note particularly the woman about to be stoned for adultery (John 8:1–11), the Samaritan woman (John 4:1–30), the woman who touches Jesus' garments (Mark 5:25–34), and many more in Luke's gospel.

___ Verse 4: According to this good saying, a noble and good woman is her husband's pride and joy—his crown! But, if she disgraces him, she is like "rot in his bones." At the risk of an accusation of being radical, what about the woman whose husband disgraces her? The answer, no doubt, is that most of the men on the "dark path" were probably married, and you can only guess at the affect on their wives and marriages.

Take Inventory

• Much of the rest of this passage deals with words and what they are capable of: treacherous advice (12:5), deadly words (12:6), delivering speech (12:6), ensnaring words (12:13). This list continues into the next passage. Wisdom involves the mind and heart, but it affects others through your words. You might want to move ahead to the New Testament for your quiet time. Read what Jesus' brother has to say about words and the tongue in James 3.

To Memorize

A good man obtaineth favour of the LORD. Proverbs 12:2

Day 7

Proverbs 12:14–28

14 A man shall be satisfied with good by the fruit of his mouth: and the recompense of a man's hands shall be rendered unto him.

15 The way of a fool is right in his own eyes: but he that hearkeneth unto counsel is wise.

16 A fool's wrath is presently known: but a prudent man covereth shame.

17 He that speaketh truth showeth forth righteousness: but a false witness deceit.

18 There is that speaketh like the piercings of a sword: but the tongue of the wise is health.

19 The lip of truth shall be established for ever: but a lying tongue is but for a moment.

20 Deceit is in the heart of them that imagine evil: but to the counselors of peace is joy.

21 There shall no evil happen to the just: but the wicked shall be filled with mischief.

22 Lying lips are abomination to the LORD: but they that deal truly are his delight.

23 A prudent man concealeth knowledge: but the heart of fools proclaimeth foolishness.

24 The hand of the diligent shall bear rule: but the slothful shall be under tribute.

25 Heaviness in the heart of man maketh it stoop: but a good word maketh it glad.

26 The righteous is more excellent than his neighbour: but the way of the wicked seduceth them.

27 The slothful man roasteth not that which he took in hunting: but the substance of a diligent man is precious.

28 In the way of righteousness is life; and in the pathway thereof there is no death.

Reflecting on Proverbs 12:14–28

recompense (12:14) reward

mischief (12:21) trouble

tribute (12:24) forced labor

seduceth (12:26) leads astray

Read and React

The Proverbs of Solomon continue their guidance in matters of the mouth, or as James says in the New Testament, "the tongue." Check out verses 14, 17–19, 22–23, and 25.

In the eighteenth century, John Keble wrote:

We scatter seed with careless hand,
*   And dream we ne'er shall see them more;*
*   But for a thousand years*
*   Their fruit appears,*
In weeds that mar the land,
*   Or helpful shore.*

The deeds we do, the words we say,—
*   Into still air they seem to fleet,*
*   We count them ever past;*
*   But they shall last,—*
In the dread judgment they
*   And we shall meet.*

___ Verse 28: Undoubtedly, the great promise of verse 28 overshadows everything else in this passage. It cries out, "Do you have any idea where the righteous way is taking you? Stay on it (or get on it!). You are on your way to where there is no death—it's everlasting life all the way!"

From this Old Testament viewpoint, what are the characteristics of those to whom everlasting life is promised? According to this chapter, it awaits those who obtain the favor of the Lord (verse 2), who are not established by wickedness (verse 3), who are virtuous (verse 4), who are pure thinking (verse 5), who possess wisdom (verse 8), who are kind to animals (verse 10), who yield fruit (verse 12), who speak good words (verse 14), who speak truth (verse 17), who give God joy and delight (verses 20, 22), who conceal knowledge (verse 23), who are industrious (verse 24), who have a glad heart (verse 25), who give good advice (verse 26), and who obtain what is precious (verse 27).

Take Inventory

• Score yourself on the fourteen characteristics of maturity above.

    1 = poor

    2 = learning

    3 = okay

    4 = good

    5 = pretty good

    6 = excellent!

What's your total score? _____

How do you interpret your score?

To Memorize

In the way of righteousness is life; and in the pathway thereof there is no death. Proverbs 12:28

WEEK FIVE
PROVERBS 13 AND 14

If the introduction to chapter 13 (verse 1) seems familiar, it's because it is. You have read those "father-son" words more than once before. Solomon is again urging us, his children, to carefully hear and understand the wisdom of this and the next chapter.

While wisdom has become a common theme, Solomon's concern for the heart, which in today's language might be considered the inner life, and the wise person's place in his world is a more personal concept. These two chapters and the next are necessary reading for twenty-first-century believers.

A Page from Contemporary Life

A few years ago on the streets of Guatemala City, there was a thirteen-year-old shoeshine boy named Jorge Maria Lopez. He was too small for his age. The heavy box he carried by a strap over his shoulders made him prematurely stooped. All that being so, he had a smile that could light up a dull day.

Each morning coming out of the Central American Hotel, I'd nearly stumble over him, standing there with one foot on his box and a smile wrapped around his face. "Shoeshine?" he'd ask me in English. At first I'd brush him off with typical American annoyance at the interruption. Then one morning I gave in and stood with my foot balanced on his box. We didn't talk much; neither of us could handle the other's language.

My shoes became the most well-shined *zapatos* south of the border. Every morning he'd be there asking, "Shoeshine?" Every morning I'd say, "Sure." By the third shine I learned that his partner in the business could speak English. That's when Jorge and I began to communicate. During each shine, I'd ask questions, which his friend Jose would translate into Spanish. Jorge was thirteen years old; he lived in a church orphanage down the street; his hometown village priest paid the cost of living and schooling there. A lady who once stayed at that hotel gave him a Bible, which he read every night. His dream was to stay in a hotel and be an *"hombre mas importante."*

My last morning in Guatemala City, I came out of the hotel, accepted Jorge's offer of a shine, put my foot on the box, and then told him I was leaving for Guadalajara, Mexico, that morning. He looked up at me with surprise. Jose let me know that Jorge felt sad that I was leaving. Then Jorge took a dog-eared notebook out of his back pocket. He searched for a pencil but couldn't find one. I gave him a Bic pen I had in my shirt pocket. He wrote his address on a page of the notebook, then ripped it out and handed it and the pen to me. I promised I'd write and gave him the pen. "Here, keep it," I told the boy.

The bellman came out with my suitcase, and the taxi drove up. I shook Jorge's hand and jumped in the backseat. As we pulled away from the hotel curb, I looked out the back window and saw the young Guatemalan entrepreneur holding the pen and watching my taxi drive away.

When I reread Proverbs 13 in preparation for this day's writing, I came across these words, which started me thinking about Jorge in Guatemala: "There is that maketh himself rich [staying in nice hotels and traveling by taxi], yet hath nothing: there is that maketh himself poor [and shines shoes on the street], yet hath great riches" (Proverbs 13:7).

Day 1

Proverbs 13:1–12

1 A wise son heareth his father's instruction: but a scorner heareth not rebuke.

2 A man shall eat good by the fruit of his mouth: but the soul of the transgressors shall eat violence.

3 He that keepeth his mouth keepeth his life: but he that openeth wide his lips shall have destruction.

4 The soul of the sluggard desireth, and hath nothing: but the soul of the diligent shall be made fat.

5 A righteous man hateth lying: but a wicked man is loathsome, and cometh to shame.

6 Righteousness keepeth him that is upright in the way: but wickedness overthroweth the sinner.

7 There is that maketh himself rich, yet hath nothing: there is that maketh himself poor, yet hath great riches.

8 The ransom of a man's life are his riches: but the poor heareth not rebuke.

9 The light of the righteous rejoiceth: but the lamp of the wicked shall be put out.

10 Only by pride cometh contention: but with the well advised is wisdom.

11 Wealth gotten by vanity shall be diminished: but he that gathereth by labor shall increase.

12 Hope deferred maketh the heart sick: but when the desire cometh, it is a tree of life.

Reflecting on Proverbs 13:1–12

Meaning, please. . .

fruit of his mouth (13:2) the fruit of their words

keepeth his mouth (13:3) guards his words

Read and React

___ Verse 1: This is an abbreviated introduction. Its purpose is to urge the hearers to pay attention to the contents of this chapter—to attend to wisdom. The rest of the passage doesn't retain the father-son allusion as the writer has done in previous passages. As we progress into this chapter and beyond, you will discover that discussions of righteousness and wickedness decrease, and God's involvement disappears, though in following chapters it comes back into prominence.

___ Verses 4–12: There is another proverb, one that Solomon never heard: "Them that has gets!" A bit cynical, perhaps, but often true. Imagine the lazybone of a sluggard you meet in verse 4. He sits up from his chaise lounge long enough to see his diligent neighbor pruning and feeding his rose garden. "Man," says the sluggard, "I wish I could grow roses like that." Then he flops back down on his lounge chair and continues his snooze.

A desire for roses is one thing, but obtaining them is something else. The story of Jorge in this week's introduction bears this out. I wrote to the young shoeshine boy in care of Santa Teresa Church, School, and Children's Home. A sister from the convent answered my letter. She told me that a distant uncle had shown up at their door and asked to take Jorge with him. Suspicious, the nuns stalled the man and began an investigation. As it turned out, he was a wealthy landowner from Honduras and indeed a blood relative of Jorge. It's almost a sure thing that Jorge Maria Lopez finally got to stay in a hotel and take a taxi ride. It is not a sure thing that the young shoeshine boy will find happiness and abundant life in his great uncle's riches. That haunts me. I keep a framed photo of Jorge shining my shoes, taken by a street photographer, in my study. I regularly talk to God about him.

___ Verse 12: "Hope deferred" is a heartbreaking phrase that describes too many of the world's people. Solomon is letting us know that hoping for a hotel stay is one thing, but the hope of abundant life is something else. From his perspective here in chapter 13, wealth is secondary to life, and life is dependant upon wisdom.

Take Inventory
• What are your hopes? List them from most anticipated to least. Now ask yourself how the Father relates to them. What are according to His will, and for which do you keep your fingers crossed? Instant gratification seems to have become our greatest desire. What's yours?

To Memorize
Hope deferred maketh the heart sick: but when the desire cometh, it is a tree of life. Proverbs 13:12

• • •

DAY 2

Proverbs 13:13–17
13 Whoso despiseth the word shall be destroyed: but he that feareth the commandment shall be rewarded.

14 The law of the wise is a fountain of life, to depart from the snares of death.

15 Good understanding giveth favor: but the way of transgressors is hard.

16 Every prudent man dealeth with knowledge: but a fool layeth open his folly.

17 A wicked messenger falleth into mischief: but a faithful ambassador is health.

Reflecting on Proverbs 13:13–17

Meaning, please. . .

dealeth with knowledge (13:16) does everything intelligently

layeth open (13:16) displays

falleth into mischief (13:17) brings trouble

Read and React

This brief passage deals directly with the Word of God. Only a king could be so sure of himself that he would select these parables. A sovereign realizes the importance of his words to his subjects. They must be obeyed. If they aren't, then there will be punishment meted out.

A wise king like Solomon knew the key to everlasting life lay in one's faithfulness to the King and His Words.

____ Verse 13, paraphrased: Whoever thinks he's bigger than God's law and despises it will be destroyed. But it's quite different for the person who holds the Lord's commandment in high regard—he will be rewarded.

____ Verse 14, paraphrased: To the wise, God's law is like a refreshing fountain of water that gives life to a thirsty soul, promising an escape from eternal death.

____ Verse 15, paraphrased: One with good sense receives the favor of God's people, but the way of the person who does not keep God's laws will be very difficult.

____ Verse 16, paraphrased: Those who are cleverly wise deal with words of knowledge, but it's the foolish person who makes a show of his folly.

____ Verse 17, paraphrased: A messenger who is up to no good can fall into trouble and perhaps misrepresent the one who sent him, but an honest courier will bring healing with the words he delivers.

A sure indication of spiritual maturity is how important the Word is in an individual's life. It has been divinely preserved for our growth in grace. We have it to read and study, not to be worshiped or kept under glass like a museum exhibit. It is to be used. In the New Testament, Paul wrote to his young friend Timothy, "All scripture is given by inspiration of God, and is profitable for doctrine, for reproof, for correction, for instruction in righteousness" (2 Timothy 3:16). Contemporary translations of this verse are closer to the Hebrew, in which the phrase "given by inspiration God" reads "is Godbreathed."

A thinker's question: "Are the sayings from Solomon's Proverbs inspired by God?" While some of these sayings show up in sacred writings of other cultures, most Jewish and Christian scholars believe that the compilers of these proverbs were directed by God to include them, and they have stood the test of helping and blessing those who read them and put them to work in their daily lives.

Take Inventory
• Though the book of Proverbs is all about wisdom, the entire Bible will make its readers wise, too. This would be a good time to find a "read through the Bible in a year" schedule and get started.

To Memorize
He that feareth the commandment shall be rewarded. Proverbs 13:13

• • •

DAY 3

Proverbs 13:18–25
18 Poverty and shame shall be to him that refuseth instruction: but he that regardeth reproof shall be honoured.

19 The desire accomplished is sweet to the soul: but it is abomination to fools to depart from evil.

20 He that walketh with wise men shall be wise: but a companion of fools shall be destroyed.

21 Evil pursueth sinners: but to the righteous good shall be repaid.

22 A good man leaveth an inheritance to his children's children: and the wealth of the sinner is laid up for the just.

23 Much food is in the tillage of the poor: but there is that is destroyed for want of judgment.

24 He that spareth his rod hateth his son: but he that loveth him chasteneth him betimes.

25 The righteous eateth to the satisfying of his soul: but the belly of the wicked shall want.

Reflecting on Proverbs 13:18–25

Meaning, please. . .

the desire accomplished (13:19) a longing or desire fulfilled

tillage (13:23) the crop fields

betimes (13:24) speedily, at times

Read and React

Solomon's proverbs often do not make a sharp distinction between poverty, unrighteousness, fools, laziness, and false witnesses. They appear to be grouped together in contrast to wisdom, righteousness, wealth, diligence, and life.

From our twenty-first-century point of view, Solomon's proverbs seem to speak in hyperbole—exaggerated in order to make a point. The moral concepts are black and white. There's no room for discussion or compromise. Well, let us be reminded that in most biblical lessons of what constitutes spiritual maturity, wise living, and certain death, there appear to be no gray areas for argumentation. Proverbs isn't philosophy, it is a no-holds-barred treatment of right and wrong.

____ Verse 19: In the other day's study you read, "Hope deferred maketh the heart sick: but when the desire cometh, it is a tree of life" (13:12). Today we return to that concept, some seven verses later, "The desire accomplished is sweet to the soul" (13:19). In other words, don't put off until tomorrow what you ought to do today. That's not hyperbole, that's common sense. It has a message to those of us who live in troubled times, when it's easier to defer decisions. Many of us still have the Scarlett O'Hara mentality: "I'll think about that tomorrow."

___ Verse 24: Surprisingly, here in a discussion about wealth and poverty, we find child-rearing advice—the proverb we have come to recite as "Spare the rod and spoil the child." In actuality, Solomon's proverb is not advocating child abuse—the rod is simply a figure of speech for any kind of discipline. He is telling parents to apply discipline in order to drive out folly, so the child will not follow the path of destruction. All discipline for any age person is rooted in love (see Proverbs 3:11–12).

Take Inventory

• From your far-removed point of view, how do these proverbs affect your life? Should they be taken with the proverbial grain of salt? In light of verse 25, where are you gaining—in the issues of your world or in your soul?

To Memorize

He that loveth him chasteneth him. Proverbs 13:24

• • •

Day 4

Proverbs 14:1–8

1 Every wise woman buildeth her house: but the foolish plucketh it down with her hands.

2 He that walketh in his uprightness feareth the LORD: but he that is perverse in his ways despiseth him.

3 In the mouth of the foolish is a rod of pride: but the lips of the wise shall preserve them.

4 Where no oxen are, the crib is clean: but much increase is by the strength of the ox.

5 A faithful witness will not lie: but a false witness will utter lies.

6 A scorner seeketh wisdom, and findeth it not: but knowledge is easy unto him that understandeth.

7 Go from the presence of a foolish man, when thou perceivest not in him the lips of knowledge.

8 The wisdom of the prudent is to understand his way: but the folly of fools is deceit.

Reflecting on Proverbs 14:1–8

Meaning, please. . .

buildeth her house (14:1) raises her family

crib (14:4) grain

Read and React

Chapter 14 opens with a four-verse introduction that again urges the reader, with an implicit challenge, to seek wisdom and avoid folly. While not the personifications from earlier chapters, Lady Wisdom and Dame Folly are represented by the two women of verse 1.

___ Verse 1: He may not have meant humor in this verse, but Solomon certainly paints a picturesque situation. Two neighbor women in bib overalls and rolled-up sleeves standing on ladders with hammers in their hands. One has nails between her lips and is framing in her new home. The other is swinging her claw hammer with great force in order to tear down her abode.

In actuality, this is no laughing matter; it is eternal truth that every parent or couple must face. Is the real you building up or tearing down your family? Of course, the important word in both instances is *wisdom*, either its presence or its absence. Neighbor Folly is tearing at the foundation as well as the superstructure, while Neighbor Wisdom is adding supports and reinforcements. She is making sure there are no cracks in the foundation.

What will build up the family? The lessons Solomon presses upon his own family:

____ Verse 2: Reverence for the Lord.

Just as no child should fear his or her parents, so none of our heavenly Father's children should fear Him, but should love and honor Him. Some who read these words do not have a father whom they admire and trust. But everyone has a Father in heaven who can be loved and trusted.

____ Verse 5: Commitment to honesty.

Truth and honesty have to be at the foundation of family living, even as it must be the underpinning for a family of one. Lying to one's self can be as damning to one's own soul as is lying to those you call loved ones and friends. All other good crumbles away when deceit is practiced in a family.

____ Verse 6: Understanding of wisdom

While good report cards should be the norm, every member of your household should understand and develop godly wisdom. Resources, family traditions, worshiping together, and times of prayer will all contribute to each one's growth in wisdom.

Take Inventory
- What are held up as requisites for successful family living have to get their start within the heart and mind of each individual within that family unit. That's the real mortar that holds the bricks of your spiritual house together. It's the fabric of any single unit dwellings, too.

To Memorize
He that walketh in his uprightness feareth the LORD. Proverbs 14:2

Day 5

Proverbs 14:9–18

9 Fools make a mock at sin: but among the righteous there is favour.

10 The heart knoweth his own bitterness; and a stranger doth not intermeddle with his joy.

11 The house of the wicked shall be overthrown: but the tabernacle of the upright shall flourish.

12 There is a way which seemeth right unto a man, but the end thereof are the ways of death.

13 Even in laughter the heart is sorrowful; and the end of that mirth is heaviness.

14 The backslider in heart shall be filled with his own ways: and a good man shall be satisfied from himself.

15 The simple believeth every word: but the prudent man looketh well to his going.

16 A wise man feareth, and departeth from evil: but the fool rageth, and is confident.

17 He that is soon angry dealeth foolishly: and a man of wicked devices is hated.

18 The simple inherit folly: but the prudent are crowned with knowledge.

Reflecting on Proverbs 14:9–18

Meaning, please. . .

mock at sin (14:9) mock at remedy for sin

intermeddle (14:10) share

tabernacle (14:11) tent

going (14:15) steps

prudent (14:18) wise and clever

Read and React

Before going any further in this study, stop and consider what would have been different if Solomon had written and collected these proverbs after Jesus Christ came into the world and ministered, then was crucified, buried, and resurrected.

____ Verse 9: The very first verse in this passage would probably have a different connotation if Solomon had known Jesus and His redemptive work. In the King James Version printed here, one phrase is "Fools make a mock at sin." In contemporary translations, in which the Hebrew has been correctly interpreted, this verse would read, "Fools ridicule making amends for sin," or "The foolish mock at the guilt offering." That is, they make fun of the animal sacrifices and the rituals that are part of it.

Had Solomon been to Mount Calvary and stood outside an empty tomb and been with the disciples when Jesus returned to heaven, he may have written Proverbs 14:9 like this: "Fools make a mockery out of the sin offering Jesus provided for us."

____ Verse 12: On Solomon's BC side of Jesus' earthly ministry, "the way" referred to here in verse 12 would have begun with wisdom. Throughout these sayings, the way of life is the way of wisdom. Had these been AD proverbs, "the way" would have been Jesus Christ.

This twelfth verse has been a favorite preaching text for preachers through the years. There is a way which seems right to the average person. But appearances can be deceitful. All the sincerity in the world will not make up for the fact that it is not God's way and that it leads to death. According to the Word, the real way to eternal life must involve a change of heart and the decision to "walk in the light."

> *If in this darksome wild I stray,*
> *Be Thou my Light, be Thou my Way.*

> —COUNT ZINZENDORF, translated by John Wesley

Take Inventory

- Return to verse 12. Spend some quiet time praying about the way in which you are traveling. Perhaps it has taken you through dark shadows and along a few stony precipices. Have you had the assurance of God's presence? When the Way has been overwhelmingly sunlit and and blessed with God's presence, have you thanked Him?

- Talk to Him about it.

To Memorize

There is a way which seemeth right unto a man, but the end thereof are the ways of death. Proverbs 14:12

• • •

DAY 6

Proverbs 14:19–26

19 The evil bow before the good; and the wicked at the gates of the righteous.

20 The poor is hated even of his own neighbour: but the rich hath many friends.

21 He that despiseth his neighbour sinneth: but he that hath mercy on the poor, happy is he.

22 Do they not err that devise evil? but mercy and truth shall be to them that devise good.

23 In all labour there is profit: but the talk of the lips tendeth only to penury.

24 The crown of the wise is their riches: but the foolishness of fools is folly.

25 A true witness delivereth souls: but a deceitful witness speaketh lies.

26 In the fear of the LORD is strong confidence: and his children shall have a place of refuge.

Reflecting on Proverbs 14:19–26

Meaning, please. . .

err (14:22) go astray

penury (14:23) poverty

delivereth souls (14:25) saves lives

Read and React

Today's Proverbs selection continues describing the prizes for those who take the way of life. Yesterday we discovered that the prudent are crowned with knowledge (14:18). Who knows if athletes in that day were as admired as they are in our day? The award of a "crown," more often than not, was for track and field men who persevered and ran the race that was set before them (Hebrews 12:1). A crown of laurel leaves, not a photo on a Wheaties box, was their reward.

____ Verse 19: There are other awards for faithfulness, perhaps not as flashy as a crown, but certainly more satisfying: "The evil bow before the good; and the wicked at the gates of the righteous."

____ Verses 20–21: And the reward for those who are poor? Their neighbors dislike and even shun them. On the other hand, the wealthy have more friends than they know what to do with. Now, Solomon has something to say to those shunning neighbors, "He who hates his neighbor is a sinner." The reward of happiness is awarded to the merciful neighbors.

____ Verse 26: Contemporary translators have given this verse such verve and promise. Such interpretations might read something like, "There is strong confidence that is fortresslike, when you give the Lord first place in your life." The paraphrase continues, "And in the fortress of your confidence, your children will find security." Amen! Hallelujah!

- It was comedian W. C. Fields, who laughingly said, "I am free of all prejudice. I hate everyone equally." It's a good one-liner for an old movie, but not too appropriate for the high road. Problem is, there is too much hate swirling all around us. We may not hate the poor, per se, but we do heartily despise stepping over street people. We are all color blind, until we pass on the choice joke we heard at work. Sexism is wrong, except when we can peek at some "artistic" pictures in a slick magazine. We know that we should love everyone, even give money to an AIDS drive, but you are certain God has something to do with the epidemic.

- What about your prejudices?

To Memorize
He that despiseth his neighbour sinneth: but he that hath mercy on the poor, happy is he. Proverbs 14:21

• • •

DAY 7

Proverbs 14:27–35

27 The fear of the LORD is a fountain of life, to depart from the snares of death.

28 In the multitude of people is the king's honour: but in the want of people is the destruction of the prince.

29 He that is slow to wrath is of great understanding: but he that is hasty of spirit exalteth folly.

30 A sound heart is the life of the flesh: but envy the rottenness of the bones.

31 He that oppresseth the poor reproacheth his Maker: but he that honoureth him hath mercy on the poor.

32 The wicked is driven away in his wickedness: but the righteous hath hope in his death.

33 Wisdom resteth in the heart of him that hath understanding: but that which is in the midst of fools is made known.

34 Righteousness exalteth a nation: but sin is a reproach to any people.

35 The king's favour is toward a wise servant: but his wrath is against him that causeth shame.

Reflecting on Proverbs 14:27–35

Meaning, please. . .

to depart from (14:27) avoiding

want of people (14:28) without people

hasty of spirit (14:29) with a temper

a sound heart (14:30) a peaceful heart (mind)

driven away (14:32) overcome (brought down)

Read and React

The heart, in scripture, is the seat of affection. All emotions symbolically involve the heart. Of course that has carried over into the twenty-first century. If the heart metaphor weren't available, where would popular love songs be?

The American Heart Association reports there were 2,111 heart transplants performed in 2002, and as many as 1,200,000 Americans had heart attacks that year. The heart, which is said to be about the size of your fist, has become symbolic not only of love, but of life itself. Through it swirls the liquid that is life itself.

No one really knows if wise old Solomon studied medicine or psychiatry, but he makes a good case for the importance of a sound heart and mind twice in this study passage.

____ Verse 30: In this first instance, the heart is considered life-giving when it is sound. Some recent translators of this verse substitute *mind* for *heart*. The Hebrew gives you a choice, "sound or peaceful heart," or "sound or peaceful mind." Both are correct, and both contribute life to the body.

____ Verse 33: Again, the heart becomes the symbol of what is good in life. In this verse it is wisdom that resides and is at home within the man and woman who have understanding. This word *understanding* has been in a number of Solomon's parables. Are *wisdom* and *understanding* synonymous?

A common dictionary definition of *understanding* includes mental grasp, comprehension, tolerance, and a harmonious relationship to.

Besides the expected "accumulated learning," another dictionary definition of *wisdom* is the "ability to discern inner qualities and relationships." That's close to Solomon's concept of wisdom—a combination of learning and spiritual discernment. It includes experience and an open heart. When compared to understanding, wisdom demands a touch of the divine.

Take Inventory

• During your quiet time, consider how wisdom and understanding affect your life. How do they both relate to your work? Is there a difference between them as you interact with your coworkers? In what ways might you be more tolerant? React to these lines:

> *Knowledge and wisdom, far from being one ,*
> *Have oft-times no connection. Knowledge dwells in heads*
> *Replete with thought of other men.*
> *Wisdom, in minds attentive to their own.*
> *Knowledge is proud that he has learn'd so much;*
> *Wisdom is humble that he knows no more.*

—WILLIAM COWPER

To Memorize

The fear of the LORD is a fountain of life, to depart from the snares of death. Proverbs 14:27

WEEK SIX
PROVERBS 15 AND 16

At this mid-point in the book of Proverbs, we once more encounter the contrast between wisdom and folly, though it's not as lively as in earlier chapters. These contrasts that we have discovered in Solomon's writings and assemblages are not unique to this setting. Most collections of "succinct and pithy sayings" contain this literary device. Proverbs are part of every spoken language and folk literature that originated in oral traditions. Every culture has highlighted some form of the battle between Good and Evil. And of course, there is an implied directive to shun the latter and make every effort to aim for the former. These verses take the reader into a new collection of wise sayings.

A Page from Contemporary Life

Buried in chapter 15 is a phrase that has opened the floodgates of memory to this writer. It's the last part of verse 11: "How much more then the hearts of the children of men?" The first half of that verse refers to hell and destruction and their relation to the Lord. It's another contrast verse.

And why does that phrase speak to me? My paraphrase of verse 11 is, "If the good Lord knows all about such a wicked place as hell, how much more He knows about my human heart and the hell it has gone through?" Biblical scholars will probably scoff at my paraphrase. But let me share something very personal with you:

I suffer from depression. Before I was willing to look for help, I caused great pain to those I love, as well as to myself. While I spoke and wrote about God's solutions to our problems, I didn't practice what I preached. Finally I sought help, which included a three-week hospital stay. At first, those were frightening hours and days. Then slowly I discovered that all that was happening was for my good. Then one morning it dawned on me: My Father is well acquainted with who I am, where I am, and what I need.

That evening a group of us were taken out to an "exercise garden." Each week we were given a timed physical problem to solve as a group. Our problem on this particular night was to get all ten of us up and over a twelve-foot wall. The very thought of taking part in this exercise chilled my blood. Everyone in this group was at least twenty-five years younger than me, not to mention more fit and less arthritic.

"What's the game plan?" someone asked.

"My plan is to sit this one out," I demurred.

"Oh no," our coach replied, "everyone goes up and over."

"Yeah, but. . ."

"Sorry, Paul, them's the rules!"

"I have an idea," Suzie-the-Small piped up, "You'll boost me up first, then one other person. When there are two of us on top, send Paul up." Can any of you who read these words understand how fat and ungainly I felt? Didn't anyone understand how scared I was?

"No time for crying, we've got twenty minutes left to solve this problem." With those words, the whole group minus Suzie formed a human pyramid. Suzie scaled the bodies, then those on top lifted her, gave her a boost, and she grabbed the top of the wall and pulled herself up. Charlie, who was bit larger than Suzie, went up next.

Then it was my turn. I scaled the bodies, which kind of collapsed under me. When I was on the apex of our pyramid, I stood on the back of the poor soul under me and leaned against the wall till I got my balance. Then with bone-jarring energy, they sort of tossed me up against the wall. I grabbed the top rail and hung there with my nose pressed against the wood. Four hands from above grabbed my wrists and pulled up while my feet shuffled against the wood. Then with a mighty "heave ho" this Moby Dick was yanked up, and over I went. I made it! Never in all my years did I ever feel such euphoria. I had succeeded. The kids still on the ground clapped and cheered. I overcame my fear!

At the debriefing, I opened up to the whole group and described my depressions and my fears. I saw Suzie-the-Small write something on paper while I was speaking. Afterwards she handed the folded paper to me. I opened it and read, "God knows all about you."

That's what the second half of Proverbs 15:11 says to me: "He know all about me—and still does."

Day 1

Proverbs 15:1–10

1 A soft answer turneth away wrath: but grievous words stir up anger.

2 The tongue of the wise useth knowledge aright: but the mouth of fools poureth out foolishness.

3 The eyes of the LORD are in every place, beholding the evil and the good.

4 A wholesome tongue is a tree of life: but perverseness therein is a breach in the spirit.

5 A fool despiseth his father's instruction: but he that regardeth reproof is prudent.

6 In the house of the righteous is much treasure: but in the revenues of the wicked is trouble.

7 The lips of the wise disperse knowledge: but the heart of the foolish doeth not so.

8 The sacrifice of the wicked is an abomination to the LORD: but the prayer of the upright is his delight.

9 The way of the wicked is an abomination unto the LORD: but he loveth him that followeth after righteousness.

10 Correction is grievous unto him that forsaketh the way: and he that hateth reproof shall die.

Reflecting on Proverbs 15:1–10

Meaning, please. . .

grievous words (15:1) harsh words

revenues (15:6) income

reproof (15:10) correction

Read and React

Words, the mouth, the tongue, and the lips all come into play in these ten verses. First of all, this selection is a reflection on the effects of thoughtful use of language, as well as a warning about its thoughtless use. Here again, we discover a foundation for James' concerns in the New Testament.

____ Verse 1: Oh, how some of us need to engrave this verse on our hearts and into our minds. The printed version here uses the term *soft* to describe an anger-changing attitude. Some others have used the word *gentle*. Either way, gentleness always makes the angered think twice.

Note the phrase "stir up anger." Doesn't that imply that anger is present somewhere down there in your heart? Perhaps this is a plea to ask the Spirit to help us control that wretched character flaw. Can we pray to have it removed?

____ Verses 2, 7: Knowing how to use knowledge is another thought provoker. Such words as blackmail, perjury, and gossip come to mind. The knowledgable tongue must learn when to tell all it knows and when not to.

____ Verse 8: "The prayer of the upright is his delight" is set in contrast to "the sacrifice of the wicked." Even when prayer is a whisper of the heart and not in the pulpit on Sunday morning, it is a reflection of Psalm 141:2: "Let my prayer be set forth before thee as incense, and the lifting up of my hands as the evening sacrifice." That's the kind of sacrifice our Father seeks.

Take Inventory

• Back to verse 1: While the contemporary translation of "harsh" for "grievous," speaks easier to modern readers, there is something about "grievous" that speaks to the human mind. It describes what harsh words do to the one who speaks them—one cannot help but grieve over the words, the attitude behind them, and eventually, what an unruly tongue has done to the other person.

• The word *soft* has such a less-than-macho or less-than-sophisticated aura about it. It's like the word *gentle*. Both have lost their power. To too many, they now reflect weakness. God help us to think twice about our need to be less than harsh.

To Memorize

A soft answer turneth away wrath: but grievous words stir up anger. Proverbs 15:1

. . .

Day 2

Proverbs 15:11–20

11 Hell and destruction are before the LORD: how much more then the hearts of the children of men?

12 A scorner loveth not one that reproveth him: neither will he go unto the wise.

13 A merry heart maketh a cheerful countenance: but by sorrow of the heart the spirit is broken.

14 The heart of him that hath understanding seeketh knowledge: but the mouth of fools feedeth on foolishness.

15 All the days of the afflicted are evil: but he that is of a merry heart hath a continual feast.

16 Better is little with the fear of the LORD than great treasure and trouble therewith.

17 Better is a dinner of herbs where love is, than a stalled ox and hatred therewith.

18 A wrathful man stirreth up strife: but he that is slow to anger appeaseth strife.

19 The way of the slothful man is as an hedge of thorns: but the way of the righteous is made plain.

20 A wise son maketh a glad father: but a foolish man despiseth his mother.

Reflecting on Proverbs 15:11–20

Meaning, please. . .

are before (15:11) lie open
afflicted (15:15) poor
stalled ox (15:17) fatted ox

Read and React

Solomon appears to be a lay psychologist in this passage—a psychologist of careful observation. Any leader of his people must have the power of observation.

___ Verse 13: "A merry heart maketh a cheerful countenance," and look ahead to 15:30, "The light of the eyes rejoiceth the heart: and a good report maketh the bones fat."

I recently enjoyed a carb-saturated Thanksgiving feast. All around our table were happy faces, but missing from our table was the son of a distant cousin. In Baghdad, he was having turkey with all the trimmings. At our table, our faces became sober as we thought of him. But what a change when the e-mail came in, and our missing marine sent his very special Thanksgiving Day greeting! How merry our hearts became! How our eyes reflected the joy we felt within!

___ Verses 16–17: Here are the two "Better than" sayings that stress times when, contrary to expected appearances, little is preferred over much. One could become skeptical as a result of these two verses. "Sure, little is much when God is in it." But why can't God be in the much, too? Don't you think you could be trusted with "great treasure"? And as far as a good meal is concerned, vegetarians probably enjoy a hearty herb soup, but as for you, wouldn't you prefer fatted ox?

No doubt, the author of these two verses realized that the man and woman on the street who read these wise sayings may not have had a fatted ox in the barn. There has been a popular theology in some Christian circles that preaches the importance of getting and having. If you don't have "great treasure" or a "fatted ox," you just haven't met the conditions. King Solomon, realist that he may have been, wanted everyone to know that we are better off with little if God is in it.

Take Inventory
• A controlled tongue and joyful contentment are hallmarks of the maturing child of God. Try this in your imagination: If you stopped each of your family members, colleagues, and friends, and asked, "Do you ever have trouble with my tongue?" or "Do I seem like a happy person?" What would their responses be?

To Memorize
A merry heart maketh a cheerful countenance. Proverbs 15:13

• • •

Day 3

Proverbs 15:21–33
21 Folly is joy to him that is destitute of wisdom: but a man of understanding walketh uprightly.

22 Without counsel purposes are disappointed: but in the multitude of counsellors they are established.

23 A man hath joy by the answer of his mouth: and a word spoken in due season, how good is it!

24 The way of life is above to the wise, that he may depart from hell beneath.

25 The LORD will destroy the house of the proud: but he will establish the border of the widow.

26 The thoughts of the wicked are an abomination to the LORD: but the words of the pure are pleasant words.

27 He that is greedy of gain troubleth his own house; but he that hateth gifts shall live.

28 The heart of the righteous studieth to answer: but the mouth of the wicked poureth out evil things.

29 The LORD is far from the wicked: but he heareth the prayer of the righteous.

30 The light of the eyes rejoiceth the heart: and a good report maketh the bones fat.

31 The ear that heareth the reproof of life abideth among the wise.

32 He that refuseth instruction despiseth his own soul: but he that heareth reproof getteth understanding.

33 The fear of the LORD is the instruction of wisdom; and before honour is humility.

Reflecting on Proverbs 15:21–33

Meaning, please. . .

purposes are disappointed (15:22) plans go awry

answer of his mouth (15:23) an apt reply

in due season (15:23) timely

establish the border of the widow (15:25) maintains widow's boundaries

light of the eyes (15:30) cheerfulness

Read and React

Here begins the section titled, "Wisdom and Reverence for God." Again we have some recurring themes: good joy and bad joy, the senses, folly, the afflicted, and more.

For our study, let's investigate "wisdom" and "reverence for God," as we find them here. These headings or topics have been set by others and are seemingly not always appropriate.

Don't take my word for it. Investigate on your own. Provide verse references or locations under the proper heading.

<u>Worship</u>   <u>Reverence for God</u>

Now, a personal paraphrase of selected verses.

___ Verse 23: Wise persons are happy when they can give an appropriate reply. Peter, in the New Testament, said it well, "Be ready always to give an answer to every man that asketh you a reason of the hope that is in you" (1 Peter 3:15).

___ Verse 24: To the wise person, the path of life leads upward, which will keep him or her from heading downward to eternal darkness. Eternal darkness is the worse kind of hell many of us can imagine. "God is light, and in him is no darkness at all" (1 John 1:5). No one wants to be where God is not!

___ Verse 30: There is nothing like another's cheerful look to make a person happy. It's the same with good news—it is able to make your whole body feel healthy!

Thank you, King Solomon, for reminding us of these truths.

Take Inventory
• At anytime in this study, write your own paraphrases of verses in the passage. You may personalize them to make each truly your own. In place of a non-specific pronoun, substitute your name. You need no knowledge of Hebrew to do this. It's a way for you to make the Word your own. Keep a quiet-time notebook in which you write your paraphrases. You might add prayer requests and answers, too.

To Memorize
The LORD is far from the wicked: but he heareth the prayer of the righteous. Proverbs 15:29

Day 4

Proverbs 16:1–15

1 The preparations of the heart in man, and the answer of the tongue, is from the LORD.

2 All the ways of a man are clean in his own eyes; but the LORD weigheth the spirits.

3 Commit thy works unto the LORD, and thy thoughts shall be established.

4 The LORD hath made all things for himself: yea, even the wicked for the day of evil.

5 Every one that is proud in heart is an abomination to the LORD: though hand join in hand, he shall not be unpunished.

6 By mercy and truth iniquity is purged: and by the fear of the LORD men depart from evil.

7 When a man's ways please the LORD, he maketh even his enemies to be at peace with him.

8 Better is a little with righteousness than great revenues without right.

9 A man's heart deviseth his way: but the LORD directeth his steps.

10 A divine sentence is in the lips of the king: his mouth transgresseth not in judgment.

11 A just weight and balance are the LORD's: all the weights of the bag are his work.

12 It is an abomination to kings to commit wickedness: for the throne is established by righteousness.

13 Righteous lips are the delight of kings; and they love him that speaketh right.

14 The wrath of a king is as messengers of death: but a wise man will pacify it.

15 In the light of the king's countenance is life; and his favour is as a cloud of the latter rain.

Meaning, please. . .

preparations of the heart (16:1) the plans of the heart

mercy and truth (16:6) loyalty and faithfulness

Read and React

This is the beginning of what Old Testament scholars have titled the "royal" collection. In the introduction chapter of this book, it is noted that there are minimal mentions of God in Proverbs. By this time, you have discovered this for yourself. Now, in 16:1–11 the name *Lord* (Yahweh) appears nine times, and *king* (possibly referring to God) appears five times. This is the reason for the "royal" designation. In most of the passages that follow, the Lord is working with man. It seems the proverb writers want to make it very clear that humankind has its place in the scheme of things, but God surely has the upper hand.

___ Verse 1: Man is responsible for preparing his mind and heart; the Lord gives man the ability to articulate those plans.

___ Verse 3: It is man's responsibility to commit the plans to the Lord, but only He will bring them to pass.

___ Verse 4: Everything that the Lord has made is for a purpose, even the wicked for the disaster that awaits them.

___ Verse 7: When a person's ways please the Lord, He makes even a person's enemies to be at peace with him or her.

___ Verse 11: The Lord is honest in the way He weighs the issues of His creation.

___ Verse 13: The delight of kings are those who speak with righteous lips, who speak truth.

Take Inventory

• Because nothing escapes God's purpose, we are confronted with the need of living life with His purpose in mind. In the New Testament, we are reminded that "All things work together for good to them that love God, to them who are the called according to his purpose" (Romans 8:28).

• How is God's purpose made manifest in you? How do others recognize it?

To Memorize

Commit thy ways works unto the LORD, and thy thoughts shall be established. Proverbs 16:3

. . .

Day 5

Proverbs 16:16–19

16 How much better is it to get wisdom than gold! and to get understanding rather to be chosen than silver!

17 The highway of the upright is to depart from evil: he that keepeth his way preserveth his soul.

18 Pride goeth before destruction, and an haughty spirit before a fall.

19 Better it is to be of an humble spirit with the lowly, than to divide the spoil with the proud.

Reflecting on Proverbs 16:16–19

Meaning, please. . .

is to depart (16:17) to avoid

keepeth (16:17) guard

Read and React

___ Verse 16: An interviewer in this morning's sports section asked a much-admired college place kicker in his senior year if he was going to be available to the NFL when he graduated.

"No," the young man answered, "I have a calling to be a public defender. I have to get to law school!"

That was a goose-bumps-on-the-arms answer. King Solomon could have used that young man's response to illustrate "How much better is it to get wisdom than gold! and to get understanding rather to be chosen than silver!"

The list of those who have shunned fame and fortune for the good of mankind is far briefer than it ought to be. Notice, Solomon doesn't supply the promise of reward for those few. He knows much of the satisfaction that comes from wisdom is inward. Reread 3:14–15.

___ Verse 17: The highway that avoids evil was seen by the prophet Isaiah who saw this same expressway: "And an highway shall be there, and a way, and it shall be called The way of holiness; the unclean shall not pass over it" (Isaiah 35:8).

Solomon and Isaiah's highway stretches from here to eternity. A prepared way for prepared people.

___ Verse 18: "Pride goeth before destruction, and an haughty spirit before a fall." Pride and haughtiness are very personal attitudes. This isn't the first time Solomon has confronted the reader with these destructive attitudes: "When pride cometh, then cometh shame" (11:2), and "The fear of the LORD is the instruction of wisdom; and before honour is humility" (15:33).

That last verse (15:33) reminds us that humility has to be in gear before wisdom can make an impact.

___ Verse 19: The discussion of pride continues with the advice "Better it is to be of an humble spirit with the lowly, than to divide the spoil with the proud." What is there to comment on here? It's better to associate with the poor than to share ill-gotten spoils with the proud and haughty. That's Solomon's advice to those of us who like to act like we're what we really aren't.

Take Inventory

- If you were asked to head up the Humility Committee and to design a self-evaluation on discovering pride and haughtiness, what kind of questions would you ask?

    How about:

    1. What was the last act of compassion you performed in total anonymity?
    2. Are you able to discipline yourself from thinking, *I could have done that, and maybe even better?*
    3. Did you ever think, *Why wasn't I asked to sing that solo in the Christmas cantata?*

    You've got the idea. What other questions might you ask?

To Memorize

And an highway shall be there, and a way, and it shall be called The way of holiness; the unclean shall not pass over it. Isaiah 35:8

• • •

Day 6

Proverbs 16:20–25

20 He that handleth a matter wisely shall find good: and whoso trusteth in the LORD, happy is he.

21 The wise in heart shall be called prudent: and the sweetness of the lips increaseth learning.

22 Understanding is a wellspring of life unto him that hath it: but the instruction of fools is folly.

23 The heart of the wise teacheth his mouth, and addeth learning to his lips.

24 Pleasant words are as an honeycomb, sweet to the soul, and health to the bones.

25 There is a way that seemeth right unto a man, but the end thereof are the ways of death.

Reflecting on Proverbs 16:20–25

Meaning, please. . .

prudent (16:21) attentive or perceptive

sweetness of the lips (16:21) pleasant speech

teacheth his mouth (16:23) makes speech judicious

addeth learning to his lips (16:23) adds persuasiveness to words

bones (16:24) body

Read and React

Communication is an act of transmitting information. That's the major concern of this passage. To make communication transmittable, there has to be information, someone to send it, and someone to receive it.

____Verses 20–21: Prudence or attentiveness and trust are starting points for hearing from God. Because God speaks to us through avenues especially tuned to our personalities and our progress in godly maturity, it is nearly impossible to write a divine communication formula that will fit all people. But Solomon is correct that "the attentive and perceptive person is tuned to the things of God." These folks are able to understand.

____ Verse 22: Understanding God is a source of unlimited satisfaction. Those who are attentive to His direction will understand the various ways He communicates. And how is that done? Among other ways, through His Word, through the truths of the natural world, at times through impressions, and through godly teachers and preachers.

___ Verse 23: Godly teachers and preachers realize that the words of their mouths and the meditations of their hearts must be acceptable in His sight. Then the Lord can use a lesson or a morning sermon to bring specific truth to a seeking, tuned-in listener. It isn't coincidence that makes you respond, "Oh, this is for me!"

___ Verse 24: Pleasant words are like peanut butter and honey on toast. They make you feel good. Wouldn't it be wonderful if our communications from the Almighty could always be warm and fuzzy? Well, they can't! There's an interesting New Testament verse (2 Timothy 4:3) that reminds us that it is possible to hear communicators who will only tell us what we want to hear. In the last days, our "itching ears" will be make us tune in to teachers and preachers who give their audiences what the people want to hear, but God does not use His teachers and clergy that way.

___ Verse 25: Those who have grown up in the evangelical church remember preachers who preached often from this text. They still do, because it is true. One of the sure signs of a lack of communication is when a receptor has his or her mind already made up. "But this is the way my family sees it," or "I'm a free spirit. I believe those BC proverbs were for a BC audience—not for a twenty-first-century activist." And to those free spirits, God communicates His sentence—death!

Take Inventory

• This is not easy to write, but if you have "itching ears," you can forget the Truth. You'll find plenty of twenty-first-century so-called spiritual communicators who will simply comfort you with what you want to hear.

• If you do not have "itching ears," do your part in sharing the message of the Good News. Communicate the New Testament theme of the Resurrection. That's the basis of the Christian message, which is Truth.

To Memorize
There is a way that seemeth right unto a man, but the end thereof are the ways of death. Proverbs 16:25

• • •

DAY 7

Proverbs 16:26–33
26 He that laboureth laboureth for himself; for his mouth craveth it of him.

27 An ungodly man diggeth up evil: and in his lips there is as a burning fire.

28 A froward man soweth strife: and a whisperer separateth chief friends.

29 A violent man enticeth his neighbour, and leadeth him into the way that is not good.

30 He shutteth his eyes to devise froward things: moving his lips he bringeth evil to pass.

31 The hoary head is a crown of glory, if it be found in the way of righteousness.

32 He that is slow to anger is better than the mighty; and he that ruleth his spirit than he that taketh a city.

33 The lot is cast into the lap; but the whole disposing thereof is of the LORD.

Reflecting on Proverbs 16:26–33

Meaning, please. . .

mouth craveth it (16:26) appetite
in his lips (16:27) his speech
froward man (16:28) perverse person
shutteth his eyes (16:30) winks
hoary head (16:31) gray hair
disposing thereof (16:33) decision

Read and React

This selection is a continuation of the "royal" collection. Again, each of these sayings deals with common, everyday experiences. For instance. . .

____ Verse 26: The laborer works very hard because if he doesn't, he'll be hungry.

____ Verse 27: The gossip is an ungodly person; he or she absolutely burns to tell what he or she knows.

____ Verse 28: A whispering and perverse person upsets people and is able to cause all sorts of dissention among them.

____ Verse 29: A neighbor can be enticed into doing all sorts of wicked things by another neighbor who has wicked intentions.

____ Verse 30: An ungodly man, with a wink of his eye and devious words, is able to bring evil to pass.

____ Verse 31: A crown of gray hair is splendid recognition of a life well-lived.

____ Verse 32: Those who are slow to become angry are to be numbered with the mighty, as is the person who can discipline his reactions.

___ Verse 33: You may cast a lot to make a decision, but don't forget, the final decision is God's.

Take Inventory

• Every one of these paraphrased proverbs has a message to the contemporary reader. The overriding message is: "God is in control," as it is so wonderfully expressed in verse 33. It is He who helps you keep control of your anger, gray hair or no gray hair; gossip is a spoiler; and those who wink at ungodly behavior will bring evil upon themselves. Solomon has held out to you some rules for living that come terribly close to where you live.

To Memorize

He that is slow to anger is better than the mighty. Proverbs 16:32

WEEK SEVEN
PROVERBS 17 AND 18

The two chapters in this week's study cover a gamut of topics—most of them relevant to us today. How can this be? It's simple—people have not changed that much since the days before Christ. Another thing—if anyone thinks Solomon and his fellow proverb writers sat in ivory towers while they dictated these pithy sayings, well, they're wrong! The subject matter was as common to the laborers and shoppers on the street as it was to the king's court and the royal family.

Maturity is no respecter of gender, rank, or age. While it has been emphasized that wisdom is the common thread that runs through these parables, godly maturation runs a close second. As a matter of fact, one can say that the mark of a maturing child of God is the motivation behind each parable. They are the "dos and don'ts" of growing up spiritually.

For this week, we will focus on the relationship between maturing and the parables in question.

A Page from Contemporary Life
I suppose each family has its own ways of measuring their children's growth.

One father in Denver has recorded the sound of his daughter's voice from her first birthday to the present. Each birthday she has wished herself a happy birthday. Today, she's in her mid-twenties, and her dad is still recording. In just a few seconds, the public radio audience heard her say, "Happy birthday to me," from one to twenty-something years.

My neighbor photographs his son every year on the back of the same stone lion in a Kansas City park for the family Christmas card.

As for my family, we used the rather prosaic door jam system. It became such a monumental part of our lives that when we changed houses, that side of the door jam had to come with us. Today, I'm not sure where it is, but the kids grew up anyway. There are other ways of charting growth. There are driving learner's permits and licenses, prom dresses and pictures, report cards, work permits, the first Social Security card, pressed corsages, letterman's sweaters and jackets, dates, auto repair bills, baptism and confirmation certificates, and all those other scrapbook items.

None of those sentimental keepsakes indicate maturity, however. Maturity is an inner growth that affects decision making, development of values, and moral decision making. That's the goal of the book of Proverbs. It's not a manual on the technique of "super church" growing, but it is readable instruction on how to become the kind of person the super church needs on its members list.

This week we are emphasizing maturity. Let's get started.

Day 1

Proverbs 17:1–7

1 Better is a dry morsel, and quietness therewith, than an house full of sacrifices with strife.

2 A wise servant shall have rule over a son that causeth shame, and shall have part of the inheritance among the brethren.

3 The fining pot is for silver, and the furnace for gold: but the LORD trieth the hearts.

4 A wicked doer giveth heed to false lips; and a liar giveth ear to a naughty tongue.

5 Whoso mocketh the poor reproacheth his Maker: and he that is glad at calamities shall not be unpunished.

6 Children's children are the crown of old men; and the glory of children are their fathers.

7 Excellent speech becometh not a fool: much less do lying lips a prince.

Reflecting on Proverbs 17:1–7

Meaning, please. . .

sacrifices (17:1) feasting

fining pot (17:3) crucible

giveth heed (17:4) pays attention

Read and React

The dictionary provides these suggestions for what it means to be mature:

(1) slow and careful consideration, (2) having completed natural growth, (3) having attained a desired state, and (4) relating to full potential.

Since we're keeping an eye on matters of spiritual maturity this week, let's look at these seven verses and find clues to inward growth:

___ Verse 1: The mature are content and contribute to a stable home life.

___ Verse 2: The mature, regardless of position in life, will have influence and will be given responsibility and reward.

___ Verse 3: The mature will be tried by the world, but he or she knows that it is the Lord's view of the heart that is important.

___ Verse 4: The mature let gossip and whispering go in one ear and out the other.

___ Verse 5: The mature man does not evaluate a person by his appearance, abilities, position in life, reputation, or what he can do for you.

___ Verse 6: The mature realize that the young and the old are worthy of attention and our affection; they, in turn, have so much to offer us.

___ Verse 7: The mature person does not put on airs.

Maturity was so well expressed by Polonius to his son. (HAMLET, Act I, scene 3)

There,—my blessing with you!
And these few precepts in thy memory
See thou character.—Give thy thoughts no tongue,
Nor any unproportion'd thought his act.
Be thou familiar, but by no means vulgar.
The friends thou hast, and their adoption tried,
Grapple them to thy soul with hoops of steel;
But do not dull thy palm with entertainment
Of each new-hatched, unfledged comrade. Beware
Of entrance to a quarrel; but being in,
Bear't that the opposed may beware of thee.
Give every man thine ear, but few thy voice:
Take each man's censure, but reserve thy judgment.

Costly thy habit as thy purse can buy,
But not expressed in fancy; rich, not gaudy:
For the apparel oft proclaims the man. . . .
Neither a borrower nor a lender be,
For loan oft loses both itself and a friend,
And borrowing dulls the edge of husbandry.
This above all: to thine own self be true,
And it must follow, as the night the day,
Thou canst not then be false to any man.

—WILLIAM SHAKESPEARE

Take Inventory

• Following Polonius's wise words, what better inventory can be taken here than to consider each line and your connection to it?

To Memorize

Excellent speech becometh not a fool: much less do lying lips a prince.
Proverbs 17:7

• • •

DAY 2

Proverbs 17:8–15

8 A gift is as a precious stone in the eyes of him that hath it: whithersoever it turneth, it prospereth.

9 He that covereth a transgression seeketh love; but he that repeateth a matter separateth very friends.

10 A reproof entereth more into a wise man than an hundred stripes into a fool.

11 An evil man seeketh only rebellion: therefore a cruel messenger shall be sent against him.

12 Let a bear robbed of her whelps meet a man, rather than a fool in his folly.

13 Whoso rewardeth evil for good, evil shall not depart from his house.

14 The beginning of strife is as when one letteth out water: therefore leave off contention, before it be meddled with.

15 He that justifieth the wicked, and he that condemneth the just, even they both are abomination to the LORD.

Reflecting on Proverbs 17:8–15

Meaning, please. . .

a gift (17:8) a bribe

covereth a transgression (17:9) forgives an offense

whelps (17:12) cubs

letteth out water (17:14) plugging up a dam

Read and React

At the heart of this lesson and the next are Solomon's concerns about the dynamics of relationships, which are often sticking points in spiritual maturity. The concrete observations in this passage focus on relationships within the family and community. In the last lesson, those potential stresses involve old age and childhood.

____ Verse 9: In this passage, Solomon suggests that the harmony of love and friendship should be practiced even if it means overlooking slights and offenses in place of talking about them.

____ Verse 10: This does not mean that we never say the hard things to people. There are those of us who used to prefer a spanking rather than be told that we had disappointed Mom. As you grow older, as much as you hate those words, you realize they have to be said.

____ Verse 14: We are also reminded that the maturing believer should not start or love quarrels. Dissent is a recurring topic in Proverbs. It is not unusual to find immaturity taking the form of stirring up trouble throughout the community and the church. There are always people who like causing trouble and unhappiness. The cause can be as varied as anger, alcohol, mockery, gossip, or just plain meanness. Solomon has referred to many of them in previous chapters. The best solution to solve immature behavior and attitudes is to withdraw from the quarrel. To the peacemaker mind, the immature continuation of a dispute does more damage than any satisfaction of "See, I told you so!" There is never a winner in any family, community, or church quarrel. Churches sometime make jokes about church splits, but there is nothing humorous at such a happening. It only reflects badly on our Lord. The spiritually mature have to become instruments of peace and forgiveness in such sad situations.

Take Inventory

• *Make me an instrument of your peace*, prayed St. Frances of Assisi. Show your maturity this week and seek peace. Write a letter to someone with whom you have had problems. You may have to let that person know that you want to forgive and want forgiveness.

To Memorize

A reproof entereth more into a wise man than an hundred stripes into a fool. Proverbs 17:10

· · ·

Day 3

Proverbs 17:16–23

16 Wherefore is there a price in the hand of a fool to get wisdom, seeing he hath no heart to it?

17 A friend loveth at all times, and a brother is born for adversity.

18 A man void of understanding striketh hands, and becometh surety in the presence of his friend.

19 He loveth transgression that loveth strife: and he that exalteth his gate seeketh destruction.

20 He that hath a froward heart findeth no good: and he that hath a perverse tongue falleth into mischief.

21 He that begetteth a fool doeth it to his sorrow: and the father of a fool hath no joy.

22 A merry heart doeth good like a medicine: but a broken spirit drieth the bones.

23 A wicked man taketh a gift out of the bosom to pervert the ways of judgment.

Reflecting on Proverbs 17:16–23

Meaning, please. . .

price in the hand (17:16) money in hand

striketh hands (17:18) pledges

exalteth his gate (17:19) builds a high gate

gift out of the bosom (17:23) concealed bribe

Read and React

We leave family interests for a while at this point in chapter 17. The primary topics here are money, love, and worldly wisdom.

____ Verse 16: Money in the hand of a fool!—a strange situation. One commentator suggested that it might mean repayment for schooling that was to impart worldly wisdom and give him some maturity. But if this person is still a fool, the stab at education didn't work.

That brings up a question—how much does formal education contribute to maturity?

____ Verse 17: This is one of the tender verses in Solomon's Proverbs:

"A friend loveth at all times." This is not a reference to romantic love. It doesn't take much imagination to suggest that Solomon grew up hearing stories about his father David's friendship with Jonathan, the son of Saul. (See 2 Samuel 1:26.) To this day, David and Jonathan are celebrated for their love and loyalty to each other.

This kind of friendship is worth finding. The phrase "at all times" can be pretty difficult. But this relationship isn't between colleagues, or neighbors, or acquaintances, or in-laws—it's between friends. And there's another mark of maturity—the capability of loving friendship.

____ Verse 22: Here is that merry or cheerful heart again, and it speaks well of the King. He wanted his subjects to have joy and merriment in their lives. It isn't difficult to conjure up mind pictures of a scowling Father God, beating up on the wicked hosts who defied Him. How good to have a poetic soul like Solomon writing of love, merriment, friendship, passion, and even children. He is to be listened to.

Take Inventory

• For some of us, remembrances of things past are *really* past! But wherever you are in years, try to recall your best friends as a child, as a student, as an adult (in addition to your spouse). What made those friendships special? What did you contribute to them? At what point did you move into a maturity that began to affect your friendships? Who is the friend you are praying for in your quiet time?

To Memorize

A friend loveth at all times. Proverbs 17:17

DAY 4

Proverbs 17:24–18:3

24 Wisdom is before him that hath understanding; but the eyes of a fool are in the ends of the earth.

25 A foolish son is a grief to his father, and bitterness to her that bare him.

26 Also to punish the just is not good, nor to strike princes for equity.

27 He that hath knowledge spareth his words: and a man of understanding is of an excellent spirit.

28 Even a fool, when he holdeth his peace, is counted wise: and he that shutteth his lips is esteemed a man of understanding.

Proverbs 18

1 Through desire a man, having separated himself, seeketh and intermeddleth with all wisdom.

2 A fool hath no delight in understanding, but that his heart may discover itself.

3 When the wicked cometh, then cometh also contempt, and with ignominy reproach.

Reflections on Proverbs 17:24–18:3

Meaning, please. . .

excellent spirit (17:27) cool spirit

shutteth his lips (17:28) keeps his mouth shut!

having separated himself (18:1) one who lives alone

intermeddleth with all wisdom (18:1) have contempt for those with sound judgment

heart may discover itself (18:2) expressing personal opinion

ignominy reproach (18:3) with dishonor comes disgrace

Read and React

We who have spent more time in the New Testament than the Old are often reminded of Jesus' teaching while reading the wisdom books, especially Solomon's Proverbs. The universal theme of parental love and disappointment has been a recurring motif throughout this collection. It doesn't take a psychobabbler to figure out that the king had had a troubled childhood, both as the son of David and Bathsheba, as well as attempting to live up to royal and prophetic expectations, which he failed to do.

And of course Jesus the Messiah came to us through David's lineage and was born in the City of David, Bethlehem.

____ Verse 25: "A foolish son is a grief to his father." If, in fact, this is a proverb that Solomon wrote, consider the memories and pictures that were dredged up as he wrote it. Where Israel saw its golden years under King David, Solomon eventually saddened the Israelites by forsaking Yahweh and worshiping the deities of his one thousand wives and concubines. He, indeed, was a foolish son.

We who live since the coming of Jesus have a decided memory of another son. Jesus reported on this young man in a parable recorded in the Gospel of Luke. Tradition has named him "The Prodigal Son" (Luke 15). This young man broke his father's heart by taking his inheritance, going to a far country, and squandering the money on riotous living.

Like any brokenhearted father, the old man prayerfully waited for his son's return. He knew there would be a homecoming. And sure enough, one day, up the dusty road came the young man to his front porch and into his father's open arms. The central message of this parable? A loving father forgives.

Take Inventory
• Read Solomon's prayer in 1 Kings 8:22–66.

To Memorize
Wisdom is before him that hath understanding. Proverbs 17:24

Day 5

Proverbs 18:4–11

4 The words of a man's mouth are as deep waters, and the wellspring of wisdom as a flowing brook.

5 It is not good to accept the person of the wicked, to overthrow the righteous in judgment.

6 A fool's lips enter into contention, and his mouth calleth for strokes.

7 A fool's mouth is his destruction, and his lips are the snare of his soul.

8 The words of a talebearer are as wounds, and they go down into the innermost parts of the belly.

9 He also that is slothful in his work is brother to him that is a great waster.

10 The name of the LORD is a strong tower: the righteous runneth into it, and is safe.

11 The rich man's wealth is his strong city, and as an high wall in his own conceit.

Reflecting on Proverbs 18:4–11

Meaning, please. . .

strokes (18:6) beating

talebearer (18:8) gossiper

waster (18:9) vandal, destroyer

conceit (18:11) imagination

Read and React

Throughout Old Testament scripture, water is a literary device that brings about immediate recognition, even to today's readers. In Solomon's time, because of its short supply, water takes on universal symbolic meaning. It bubbles merrily in streams and brooks, lies quietly in deep pools, crashes menacingly on rocks, and bursts forth as wellsprings and fountains.

____ Verse 4: In today's passage, the water simile shows up again. This time the waters are in contrast. "Deep waters" describes words, either profound, or perhaps murky and muddled. There is no question about the meaning of the contrasting water. This latter water flows into the streambed from a fresh spring bursting out of the ground like a fountain. There is nothing murky about this description; it's a picture of wisdom—words that refresh and bring life to a parched soul.

Two other descriptive similes appear in this selection: a snare and a protective city.

____ Verse 7: "A fool's. . .lips are the snare of his soul." As opposed to a mechanical trap, the snare is a device that entangles the unsuspecting with a noose or a net. The fool's words are often not spoken to hurt, but because he is a fool, he babbles on. While those words can be hurtful to the receiver, they ensnare the heart of the fool. His thoughtless profanity, racial slurs, sexual jokes, gossip, and profane pronouncements will be his destruction.

____ Verses 10–11: There is safety and protection in the person of the Lord. While the text reads "the name of the LORD is a strong tower" it must be remembered that in scripture the "name" represents the very nature of the person himself.

On the other hand, in verse 11, "his strong city," and "an high wall" represent the supposed impregnable power of wealth. Of interest here, Solomon does not condemn the wealthy man, but there is an implication that he is misplacing his trust. According to the writer, the rich man's belief that he has security in his wealth is merely a figment of his own conceits—his imagination. High walls and strong cities will not protect the unrighteous, with or without riches.

Jesus, in all His simplicity, comments some thousand years later, "Lay up for yourselves treasures in heaven. . . . For where your treasure is, there your heart will be also" (Matthew 6:20–21).

Take Inventory

- So, what are the treasures that can be "laid up in heaven"? If you can't take it with you, what do you "lay up for yourself in heaven"? And those wise words that flow forth like a brook, do they in any way contribute positively to your "storehouse" in heaven? If Solomon were writing a specific Proverb with you in mind, what would he write? Write it in your quiet time.

To Memorize

The name of the LORD is a strong tower: the righteous runneth into it, and is safe. Proverbs 18:10

• • •

Day 6

Proverbs 18:12–19

12 Before destruction the heart of man is haughty, and before honour is humility.

13 He that answereth a matter before he heareth it, it is folly and shame unto him.

14 The spirit of a man will sustain his infirmity; but a wounded spirit who can bear?

15 The heart of the prudent getteth knowledge; and the ear of the wise seeketh knowledge.

16 A man's gift maketh room for him, and bringeth him before great men.

17 He that is first in his own cause seemeth just; but his neighbour cometh and searcheth him.

18 The lot causeth contentions to cease, and parteth between the mighty.

19 A brother offended is harder to be won than a strong city: and their contentions are like the bars of a castle.

Reflecting on Proverbs 18:12–19

Meaning, please. . .

gift maketh room (18:16) bribes open doors

searcheth him (18:17) cross-examines him

the lot (18:18) casting lots

Read and React

Our concern with spiritual maturity finds a home here in this discussion of strength and power, which began in the previous selection, with the discussion of the fortified city. Now it continues in verse 12 with an added warning about pride.

____ Verse 12: "Before destruction the heart of man is haughty." He is a veritable tower of strength. He can take on anyone or any thing. He lines up all his toys and piously testifies at church, "The Lord has really blessed me!" But way down deep, he is sure that it was his own cleverness that brought about his success.

The fly in the ointment, though, is that there is a second phrase in Proverbs 18:12: "Before honour is humility." That is, before he is respected and folks are willing to take him seriously, he will have to be "baptized" in humility.

____ Verse 16: To be faithful to this scripture, one shouldn't make the man in verse 12 appear here in verse 16, but it's such a temptation. We are told that the Verse-12-Man was haughty before his downfall. What if he were the man who used bribery to open doors and gain the ears of people who could help his cause? And let's just say his neighbor found out about the underhanded way he was making a killing on the stock market, and tipped off the authorities.

____ Verse 17: Then, let's just say that our Verse-12-Man is called into court for ill-gotten riches, and he is the first to testify on his own behalf. Why, it's all so clear—it's obvious that he is innocent of any dishonesty. But then the neighbor and the influential man turn evidence against him, and the prosecution cross-examines him, causing him to be found guilty of bribery.

Where's our boastful Verse-12-Man now? As foreseen by Solomon, he is humiliated and brought down to where he belongs. No longer can he take refuge in his riches and find strength is his wealth. It's really too bad for anyone to face such punishment in order to find godly humility.

Oh yes, one more thing. . .

____ Verse 19: "A brother offended is harder to be won than a strong city." Does Verse-12-Man fit this description? What will it take to renew relationships with him?—after he's released, of course. Think about it.

Take Inventory
• Whether or not Verse-12-Man fits the premise of verse 19 above, it is necessary to see him redeemed. In New Testament parlance, we want to see him won to the kingdom of God. All of us have a Verse-12-Man in our lives—someone who has been ostracized and punished in some way but who needs the Lord. Too simplistic? Maybe so, but when the proud are made low, there needs to be someone there to help pick them up.

To Memorize
The ear of the wise seeketh knowledge. Proverbs 18:15

• • •

DAY 7

Proverbs 18:20–24
20 A man's belly shall be satisfied with the fruit of his mouth; and with

the increase of his lips shall he be filled.

21 Death and life are in the power of the tongue: and they that love it shall eat the fruit thereof.

22 Whoso findeth a wife findeth a good thing, and obtaineth favour of the LORD.

23 The poor useth intreaties; but the rich answereth roughly.

24 A man that hath friends must shew himself friendly: and there is a friend that sticketh closer than a brother.

Reflecting on Proverbs 18:20–24

Meaning, please. . .

filled (18:20) satisfied

useth intreaties (18:23) pleads for mercy

roughly (18:23) harshly

Read and React

Here again is a wide spread of themes and topics. In five verses we are introduced to eating, parts of the body, marriage, the poor, and friendships. In all honesty, it sounds as if we are breezing through five volumes of the *Encyclopedia Britannica*!

Actually, there is a common denominator, besides the obvious (authorship, location, etc.). That commonality is satisfaction (verse 20). Perhaps the most familiar references to satisfactions is found in Psalm 91:16: "With long life I will satisfy him, and shew him my salvation."

___ Verse 20: Here in Proverbs, the satisfaction discussed is not as beautifully expressed as those found in Psalms. A man's full belly may sound a bit crude to us, but all of us know what a good meal will do for attitudes and relationships. Not a word about carbs, calories, or conditioning exercise. It's a celebration of the goodness of God.

___ Verse 21: This is a frightening thought: The human tongue is capable of controlling life and death. The same tongue that sends a message to our brain about the goodness of strawberry shortcake is the same organ that can declare the death sentence.

___ Verse 22: Now here is an example of satisfaction at its best—marriage! That's a good thing. And that good thing is even better when the marriage is blessed and favored by the Lord.

___ Verse 23: What kind of satisfaction do the poor experience when pleading for mercy? And what satisfaction does a rich person experience when he roughly tosses a few coins in the humble man's direction? Solomon implies that each person is satisfied. The homeless in his misery can say, "Thank God I'm not like him." And the wealthy man can say, "Thank God I'm not like him."

___ Verse 24: There are some people who are more companions than friends. The word for "friend" used here includes a variation of the word for "love." Companions can just play at being friends. They might include those we've come to call "fair weather friends." So where's the satisfaction in friendship? It's in that friend who's beside you through thick and thin. The Word describes him or her as "a friend that sticketh closer than a brother." There are few things more satisfying than a friendship that allows for growth and discovery, as well as companionship. Not so incidentally, that makes for a good marriage relationship, too.

Take Inventory
• In your quiet time, do a "satisfaction check." Are you satisfied with your relationship to those close to you? Are they with you? And most of all, what about that "friend that sticketh closer than a brother"—the Lord Jesus Christ?

To Memorize
There is a friend that sticketh closer than a brother. Proverbs 18:24

WEEK EIGHT
PROVERBS 19 AND 20

So, what do you think of Proverbs? It's a bit overwhelming in its coverage, isn't it? There's very little that its thirty-one chapters don't cover. Because there is no narrative or linear organization to the material, it seems to be a bit like one of Grandma's patchwork quilts—the kind that has no pattern but carries fabric pieces gathered from here and there and everywhere.

Now understand, that crazy quilt imagery is not an insult of Solomon's work, it's the recognition that BC thinking and organization doesn't register the same in the twenty-first century. At the same time, a spiritually maturing reader stumbles over truth that is just as contemporary today as it was thousands of years ago.

A Page from Contemporary Life

Perusing ahead at the contents of this week's studies in Proverbs, I see that honoring parents appears on days two and seven. That topic strikes a hugely responsive chord in me—not for my son and daughter to honor me, but for me, as a son, to celebrate my mom and dad.

I just completed volume 1 of my autobiography—the first twenty-five years of my life. It's going to be a Christmas present for my kids.

Because I can recall many details of my childhood, the writing of those early days was relatively easy, especially with the boxes of photographs I've inherited, thanks to my mother's sense of history. Trouble is, I neglected to ask her who all those people were posed so decorously clothed on beach blankets in the sand or hiding behind the twenty-pound turkey at some Thanksgiving dinner table, or lined up and towering over me in front of houses I've never seen before.

My mother died before I was able to get everyone identified. Frankly, I don't think she could have dredged up some of the names herself. And Dad, who died some twenty years before my mother, would have been no help at all.

The overriding impression I am left with after pecking out 109 pages with three fingers, is that my post-depression, World War II parents had my best interests at heart when they raised me. Dad always had a job. He was a sign painter for an oil company. And Mom never worked after I was born. She was a genuine June Cleaver mom, minus the pearls.

My dad called himself an atheist. He never went to church, but Mom saw to it that she and I went every Sunday. When we became evangelicals, there were more church services to go to—all week long—without dad.

Dad died in 1981 from throat cancer. He was a two-and-three-pack-a-day smoker. His last week, I flew from Kansas City to the San Francisco Bay Area and sat on the edge of his bed in the Walnut Creek hospital. He could not speak. Mom had gone home for lunch. I breathed a silent prayer for courage and asked him if he knew God loved him. There was a long pause. I told him to nod his head if he believed it. Dad nodded his head. Then I said, "Dad, can you accept God's love right now, and love Him back?" Again, there was a long pause. Then dad nodded his head.

I'm not sure if mom ever believed my story of Dad accepting God's love while she was eating lunch. But it happened just as I report it. And when mom was dying in a nursing facility here in Kansas City, she kept talking to dad in her delirium. I believe he was getting her ready to join him. For all of the foregoing and so much more, I thank God for my parents.

DAY 1

Proverbs 19:1–8

1 Better is the poor that walketh in his integrity, than he that is perverse in his lips, and is a fool.

2 Also, that the soul be without knowledge, it is not good; and he that hasteth with his feet sinneth.

3 The foolishness of man perverteth his way: and his heart fretteth against the LORD.

4 Wealth maketh many friends; but the poor is separated from his neighbour.

5 A false witness shall not be unpunished, and he that speaketh lies shall not escape.

6 Many will intreat the favour of the prince: and every man is a friend to him that giveth gifts.

7 All the brethren of the poor do hate him: how much more do his friends go far from him? he pursueth them with words, yet they are wanting to him.

8 He that getteth wisdom loveth his own soul: he that keepeth understanding shall find good.

Reflecting on Proverbs 19:1–8

Meaning, please. . .

hasteth with his feet (19:2) moves too hurriedly

fretteth (19:3) rages

go far from him (19:7) shuns

Read and React

In these eight verses, the poor are discussed at least three times. In Solomon's day, the poor were everywhere. Because there was no so-called middle class, you were either on the top or the bottom of the social ladder. When you were at the bottom, you discovered there were no rungs going up.

None of the poverty proverbs in this book shame the poor, unless the poverty has come about because of laziness. Solomon and his fellow writers had no time for slothfulness. The lazy individual deserved all unhappiness.

___ Verse 1: It is possible to be poor and yet walk with integrity. The elderly lady in the grocery store line the other day was obviously embarrassed to hand food stamps to the cashier. "I've never had to do this before," she said.

The young woman at the register replied, "Let's thank God that you have these stamps."

Try to imagine a society with no social responsibility outside its own class. That is how it was in those BC days.

___ Verses 4, 7: A contrast parable: While wealth gathers many friends, "the poor is separated from his neighbour." Modern translations of this verse are quite up-front about its meaning, "A poor person's friends desert him."

There was a time when the church appeared to be more involved with the poor overseas than in its own backyard. Today, thank God, that is changing, especially among the young. In churches all across North America, young people and their leaders are developing social consciences. In Kansas City, youth groups are making weekly visits to the transients who sleep under the Missouri River bridges. Their ministry is to distribute blankets and sandwiches to the transients who sleep there every night of the year.

It was Jesus who said, "Inasmuch as ye have done it unto one of the least of these my brethren, ye have done it unto me" (Matthew 25:40).

Take Inventory

• How would you relate Jesus' words above to the three poverty verses in this passage? What does Jesus' word "it" mean to you? What would it mean in Solomon's day?

To Memorize
Inasmuch as ye have done it unto one of the least of these my brethren, ye have done it unto me. Matthew 25:40

. . .

DAY 2

Proverbs 19:9–18
9 A false witness shall not be unpunished, and he that speaketh lies shall perish.

10 Delight is not seemly for a fool; much less for a servant to have rule over princes.

11 The discretion of a man deferreth his anger; and it is his glory to pass over a transgression.

12 The king's wrath is as the roaring of a lion; but his favour is as dew upon the grass.

13 A foolish son is the calamity of his father: and the contentions of a wife are a continual dropping.

14 House and riches are the inheritance of fathers: and a prudent wife is from the LORD.

15 Slothfulness casteth into a deep sleep; and an idle soul shall suffer hunger.

16 He that keepeth the commandment keepeth his own soul; but he that despiseth his ways shall die.

17 He that hath pity upon the poor lendeth unto the LORD; and that which he hath given will he pay him again.

18 Chasten thy son while there is hope, and let not thy soul spare for his crying.

Meaning, please. . .

delight (19:10) luxury

discretion (19:11) good sense

pass over (19:11) overlook

contentions (19:13) quarreling

continual dropping (19:13) dripping rain

Read and React

With conflict at the heart of this study selection, you are given an excellent yardstick against which to measure your current state of maturity. How so? It can be nicely illustrated by the old sermon story about a wayward grain of sand that gets transported between the shells of an unsuspecting oyster and scratches its tender tummy to the point where the oyster emits a lubricant that eases the itch and makes the grain a gleaming white pearl.

Maturing believers should be able to take any conflicting situation and turn it bearable, if not a pearl! For instance:

____ Verse 11: A paraphrase of this verse might read, "If you have good sense, you will overlook an offense; after all, such an action will give you character. It's to your benefit that you are slow to anger." Anger is not a vice, unless it injures others or yourself. You are usually able to control conflict by controlling yourself. Think of a quarrelsome situation as another opportunity to stretch toward maturity.

____ Verse 13: Family conflict has been the target of jokes and television sitcoms, yet there is nothing humorous about derailed relationships, especially between a parent and a child. Both parties can assume either role. Believe it or not, there are certainly times when a son or daughter is the more mature person. "Dads, don't provoke your children to wrath," says Paul in Ephesians 6:4. In that same

Ephesians chapter, he advises, "Children, obey your parents in the LORD: for this is right" (6:1).

Then there are husbands and wives! Solomon's proverb makes the villain out of the wife. Yes, there was a male bias in BC days. Nonetheless, a quarreling spouse of either gender is a major irritant in any marriage. With humor, the proverb writer compares such behavior to a steady dripping of rain.

___ Verse 18: Discipline is an indication of love—let's not forget it. In the heat of argument, when cool heads don't appear to be winning out, "let not thy soul spare for his crying." A paraphrase based on modern translations of this verse is important: "While there is yet hope, be sure to discipline your child. But, set limits to that discipline. Don't lose your cool and do harm to him or her."

Take Inventory
• Read Matthew 18:15–20 in a modern English version. This is the method Jesus established to resolve conflict within the church. A variation of it can work within a family, an office, a school class, whatever. If you are looking toward being a mature child of God, then be an instrument of His peace.

To Memorize
A prudent wife is from the LORD. Proverbs 19:14

DAY 3

Proverbs 19:19–27

19 A man of great wrath shall suffer punishment: for if thou deliver him, yet thou must do it again.

20 Hear counsel, and receive instruction, that thou mayest be wise in thy latter end.

21 There are many devices in a man's heart; nevertheless the counsel of the LORD, that shall stand.

22 The desire of a man is his kindness: and a poor man is better than a liar.

23 The fear of the LORD tendeth to life: and he that hath it shall abide satisfied; he shall not be visited with evil.

24 A slothful man hideth his hand in his bosom, and will not so much as bring it to his mouth again.

25 Smite a scorner, and the simple will beware: and reprove one that hath understanding, and he will understand knowledge.

26 He that wasteth his father, and chaseth away his mother, is a son that causeth shame, and bringeth reproach.

27 Cease, my son, to hear the instruction that causeth to err from the words of knowledge.

Reflecting on Proverbs 19:19–27

Meaning, please. . .

deliver him (19:19) bail him out

hear counsel (19:20) listen to advice

latter end (19:20) future

devices (19:21) human-made plans

in his bosom (19:24) in the dish

wasteth (19:26) do violence

Read and React

Here we go again with more on violence, then we shift gears and once again consider the benefits of wisdom. Wisdom is the reason we have this book. And many of the proverbs that don't deal directly with wisdom imply that their practice will help us acquire wisdom—maturity. But first, another violence verse:

___ Verse 19: We will always have the hot-tempered person with us. Solomon's solution for dealing with such a person is to penalize him. If you are content to walk on eggshells or tiptoe around him, you will see no improvement in that angry individual. And, if you bail him out, it's a proven fact that you'll have to do it over and over again.

__ Verses 20–21: Now, to wisdom. These words of verse 20 sound just like a parent's advice when sending Junior off to college: "Son, listen to *wise* advice, and don't close your ears to instruction, so that you will gain wisdom for the future."

Then mother adds, "Of course, dear, what your father didn't say: You're a human being, so your mind will make all sorts of plans, but please, dear, remember that it's the Lord who imparts His will for your life."

___ Verse 23: As the college-bound son finishes packing, Mom offers one more bit of advice: "In the fear and respect of our Lord, you will find abundant life, and you will feel content and secure and untouched by trouble."

Carrying his luggage down the stairs, the son pauses a moment, giving Dad an opening to add one more Solomon proverb, "Let me say one more thing, son. . . ."

___ Verse 27: "Cease straying from these words of knowledge. I want you to be able to hear instruction."

Without answering, the son drags his suitcase out the front door in his search for wisdom.

Take Inventory

- In your quiet time today, consider your plans and designs versus what the Lord might have planned for you. Take a spiritual hearing test and discover if your ears are attuned to His instruction. Reread today's study scripture.

To Memorize

The fear of the LORD tendeth to life; and he that hath it shall abide satisfied; he shall not be visited with evil. Proverbs 19:23

• • •

DAY 4

Proverbs 19:28–20:5

28 An ungodly witness scorneth judgment: and the mouth of the wicked devoureth iniquity.

29 Judgments are prepared for scorners, and stripes for the back of fools.

Proverbs 20

1 Wine is a mocker, strong drink is raging: and whosoever is deceived thereby is not wise.

2 The fear of a king is as the roaring of a lion: whoso provoketh him to anger sinneth against his own soul.

3 It is an honour for a man to cease from strife: but every fool will be meddling.

4 The sluggard will not plow by reason of the cold; therefore shall he beg in harvest, and have nothing.

5 Counsel in the heart of man is like deep water; but a man of understanding will draw it out.

Reflecting on Proverbs 19:28–20:5

Meaning, please. . .

ungodly witness (19:28) corrupt (worthless) witness

raging (20:1) brawler

fear (20:2) dreaded anger (wrath)

meddling (20:3) quarrel

counsel in the heart (20:5) purposes in the human mind

Read and React

There is nothing pointless about wisdom. The wise are able to cut through the excesses and get to the heart of the matter.

___ Verse 29: Cutting to the chase, the proverb writer lays the facts on the table: The wise are not scorners or fools, else they'd be condemned and flogged. Seems a bit intolerant, doesn't it? If this were a contemporary attitude, the ACLU would be hauling the whipping boys off to court. You'll remember that proverb writers often used hyperbole to make a point.

___ Verse 1: Solomon says right out, "Wine is a mocker, strong drink is raging," or causes one to be a brawler. He then hurries on to say, "Whosoever is deceived into thinking otherwise is not wise." There is an implication here that booze contributes to unrighteousness. Its misuse certainly contributes to the unrighteousness of broken homes, deathly accidents, and uncontrollable behavior.

___ Verse 4: Do you remember the children's story about the little red hen who wanted to bake some bread and asked various farmyard animals to give her a hand? All were too lazy or full of ridiculous excuses, so no one helped her. But, when she removed the fresh bread from the oven, all of the animals were at her front door. If you remember, because they wouldn't help, they got no warm bread and butter. Does verse four need any more wisdom explanation?

Take Inventory

- After watching the Kansas Chiefs lose their fifth football game in a row, I went out to walk Giaco, my miniature Schnauzer. My neighbor was walking his Black Lab, Candy. When Giaco spied Candy, he nearly pulled the leash out of my hand as he took out after her with out-of-character snarls. My neighbor remarked that he wished the Chiefs had shown as much ferocity. *Yeah,* I thought, *but my dog's bravery was all show. If he were wiser, he'd not tangle with a Black Lab three times his size!*

    Lord, what we need above most things is the wisdom to be our redeemed selves—not to rely on stimulants of any kind to try to make us what we aren't. Give us the maturity to know what to do, and then have the courage to do it. Amen.

To Memorize

The just man walketh in his integrity: his children are blessed after him. Proverbs 20:7

· · ·

Day 5

Proverbs 20:6–16

6 Most men will proclaim every one his own goodness: but a faithful man who can find?

7 The just man walketh in his integrity: his children are blessed after him.

8 A king that sitteth in the throne of judgment scattereth away all evil with his eyes.

9 Who can say, I have made my heart clean, I am pure from my sin?

10 Divers weights, and divers measures, both of them are alike abomination to the LORD.

11 Even a child is known by his doings, whether his work be pure, and whether it be right.

12 The hearing ear, and the seeing eye, the LORD hath made even both of them.

13 Love not sleep, lest thou come to poverty; open thine eyes, and thou shalt be satisfied with bread.

14 It is naught, it is naught, saith the buyer: but when he is gone his way, then he boasteth.

15 There is gold, and a multitude of rubies: but the lips of knowledge are a precious jewel.

16 Take his garment that is surety for a stranger: and take a pledge of him for a strange woman.

Reflecting on Proverbs 20:6–16

Meaning, please. . .

blessed (20:7) happy

divers weights, measures (20:10) different balance scale weights and measures

it is naught (20:14) it's no good!

surety (20:16) security

strange (20:16) foreign

Read and React

There are various definitions for the word *righteousness*. Some are dependent on the sacrifice of Jesus Christ, but of course, in those BC days in which Proverbs was written and collected, there was no knowledge of Calvary and the Resurrection. Still, there were Old Testament characters described as righteous. Solomon holds up some of the characteristics of Old Testament righteousness. Frankly, they represent what is expected of AD believers.

___ Verse 6: Faithfulness is the positive characteristic mentioned here. It certainly is not the blowhard attitude of the individual pictured.

___ Verse 7: Integrity is the next characteristic. The proverb again picks up the imagery of walking, which we know is a metaphor for living and being. The results? His children will happily follow him. Every person wants to be able to influence his or her child for good. According to this proverb, integrity breeds integrity. Our children are looking to us to model integrity.

___ Verse 9: Another characteristic of righteousness is dependence upon the Lord. Rhetorical questions in Hebrew wisdom literature generally expect a negative response. Of course, no one can make his own heart pure. Only God can spiritually clean up a human life.

___ Verse 11: There is something about a child's transparency that is refreshing. Certainly another mark of a righteous adult is that same "What you see is what I am" transparency.

___ Verse 12: The righteous keep their ears and eyes open to communication from the Lord and for opportunities to reach out to another person.

Take Inventory

• Is there a way to rank these characteristics of righteousness? Probably not. There is no way that one can be more important than another. All are part of godly maturity.

   Transparency is one of the truly engaging items in the above list. To be able to say, "What you see is what I am," is refreshing. All of us at various times have felt like we've needed to hide some issue in our life. Then, what a total relief it was when we finally came clean. In your quiet time, talk to your Father about this issue in your life.

To Memorize

Even a child is known by his doings, whether his work be pure, and whether it be right. Proverbs 20:11

DAY 6

Proverbs 20:17–22

17 Bread of deceit is sweet to a man; but afterwards his mouth shall be filled with gravel.

18 Every purpose is established by counsel: and with good advice make war.

19 He that goeth about as a talebearer revealeth secrets: therefore meddle not with him that flattereth with his lips.

20 Whoso curseth his father or his mother, his lamp shall be put out in obscure darkness.

21 An inheritance may be gotten hastily at the beginning; but the end thereof shall not be blessed.

22 Say not thou, I will recompense evil; but wait on the LORD, and he shall save thee.

Reflecting on Proverbs 20:17–22

Meaning, please. . .

bread of deceit (20:17) bread gained by deceit

purpose (20:18) plan

recompense (20:22) repay

Read and React

Here it is, a semi-official Solomon listing of a few very unsociable behaviors, some bad attitudes, and a couple of out-and-out breakings of the commandments. All in all, at this point, the book of Proverbs is dealing with everyday issues that are the antithesis of maturity.

___ Verse 17: Deceit. It is plain that the proverb writer is not talking about outright lying or bearing false witness. He is implying that there are so-called sweet deceits—ways of "getting off the hook," or not telling everything you know, or shading what you are really thinking. For a moment, your deceit might make a situation easier. Eventually, though, your tasty words will become gravel in your mouth. Maturity provides courage to deal honestly with a difficult situation.

____ Verse 19: Gossip. Talebearing is not the sin of only one of the genders; it is the tasty morsel that both men and women of any generation enjoy sharing. It elevates the news bearers as elite folks who are on an inside track. It makes them feel better about themselves, because they are certainly above such behavior.

____ Verse 20: Dishonoring parents. Cursing one's parents seems to be another proverb hyperbole. Who, in his right mind, would commit such a blatant act? It slaps in the face those who have given him life and sustenance. The reward for honoring parents? Long life. The reward to this one who cursed his parents? He shall be snuffed out to abide in utter darkness.

____ Verse 22: Revenge. "Vengeance is mine, I will repay; saith the Lord" (Romans 12:19).

"Yes, I know, Lord, but I would get such satisfaction out of giving her her comeuppance!"

So, who needs to be punished? The person who did harm to you, or you who want to get even? The Lord won't allow us satisfaction under those conditions. "Never fear," He tells us, "I'll take care of it according to My schedule. After all, there may be some angles that you know nothing about, and I do. Trust Me to have your best interests in mind."

Spiritual maturity brings with it patience, and patience is a sign of trust. Look back at Proverbs 3:5. This is what you'll read, "Trust in the LORD with all thine heart; and lean not unto thine own understanding."

Take Inventory
• Grade yourself (A, B, C, D, F) on each of the four transgressions above. Decide where you may need improvement. Make it a matter of quiet-time meditation and prayer.

To Memorize

Trust in the LORD with all thine heart; and lean not unto thine own understanding. Proverbs 3:5

. . .

DAY 7

Proverbs 20:23–30

23 Divers weights are an abomination unto the LORD; and a false balance is not good.

24 Man's goings are of the LORD; how can a man then understand his own way?

25 It is a snare to the man who devoureth that which is holy, and after vows to make enquiry.

26 A wise king scattereth the wicked, and bringeth the wheel over them.

27 The spirit of man is the candle of the LORD, searching all the inward parts of the belly.

28 Mercy and truth preserve the king: and his throne is upholden by mercy.

29 The glory of young men is their strength: and the beauty of old men is the gray head.

30 The blueness of a wound cleanseth away evil: so do stripes the inward parts of the belly.

Reflecting on Proverbs 20:23–30

Meaning, please. . .

devourereth that which is holy (20:25) rashly say something is holy

after vows, enquiry (20:25) the reflection after making vows

scattereth (20:26) winnows (like chaff)

belly (20:27) innermost part

Read and React

After the previous lesson's negative turn, this passage of Proverbs provides us a balance lesson—three negative issues and three positive characterstics that contribute to spiritual maturity.

Hindrances to Spiritual Maturity:

___ Verse 23: Cheating. Cutting corners appears to be a hallmark of our age, and not just in commercial matters. It's in the classroom, the pharmacy, at church, on the ballfield, in the home. Might it be a conspiracy to give all the appearance of fairness while shaving a bit off in order to look good or earn a little extra? The English say, "Who cheats in small things is a fool; in great things, a rogue."

___ Verse 24: Bullheadedness. Some will call this quality "stick-to-it-ness," but Solomon looks at it differently. To him, it is illustrated by a person trying to tell God which way he should go, while all along it is God who calls the shots and directs the path.

___ Verse 25: Speaking impetuously. In this description of a hindrance to maturity, Solomon paints the picture of a man entrapped by his action—he made a promise to the Lord, perhaps to pledge a sum of money or his time to the church. His motivation to do it may have been emotion, or it may have been to look good. At any rate, he made the vow too quickly and ends up questioning his vow. Better to take the pledge card home and pray over it.

Positive Helps to Maturity:

___ Verse 27: A lamp of the Lord. Remember that Sunday school song that goes, "This little light of mine, I'm gonna to let it shine. . . ."? Did you realize that gleaming lamp is the Spirit of the Lord that's within you? This proverb is a reminder that the light is continually burning in order to "search out" all the hidden parts of your mind, your heart—in fact, all of you. You are fortunate to have the Spirit's presence in your life.

____ Verse 28: Mercy and truth. In some modern versions of this verse, the translators have selected love and faithfulness as the qualities necessary for maturity. Whichever, all four of them are appropriate.

____ Verse 29: Beauty of youth and age. The glory of the young *is* their strength. It's their ability to dream dreams, their desire to make a difference in their world. And the older generation? "The beauty of old men is the gray head." Their age and experience deserve attention and respect.

Take Inventory
• Spend time considering Proverbs 20:28. Check out some Old and New Testament verses on these topics:

> Mercy: Psalm 23:6; Luke 1:50; Ephesians 2:4
>
> Truth: Psalm 51:6; Luke 1:14; Ephesians 4:15
>
> Love: Deuteronomy 6:5; 1 Corinthians 13; 1 John 4

To Memorize
The spirit of man is the candle of the LORD. Proverbs 20:27

WEEK NINE

Hopefully by this time in your study of Proverbs you have observed that there appear to be three social backgrounds from which these "pithy sayings" emerge: the heart of the family, the royal court and its school, and the classrooms of theological training.

Because the home is the natural place for teaching the lessons of life, much of what you read in these thirty-one chapters reflects hearthside teaching—or at least the lessons are couched in that milieu. These are the father-son lessons. On another level, the king's court and its school comes into play. In the Middle Eastern world, wisdom teaching was officially the province of the court schools. Thirdly, some of the proverbs reflect theological questions and observations, such as creation and revelation (see 3:19–20; 8:22–31; 30:2–6).

A Page from Contemporary Life

I did my seminary training in Berkeley, California, and also worked on a Master's degree in English at the university. Talk about extreme points of view! Besides this, I was unmarried and lived at home with my parents. Hence, I have firsthand knowledge about learning from the hearthstone, liberal arts classrooms, and theology professors—all at the same time! Here are a few proverbs I'd like to toss into Solomon's hopper.

- You are not maturing if you limit your associations to those with whom you already see eye-to-eye; you may be setting old prejudices into concrete.

- There is no *U* in wisdom, there is only an *I*; my first responsibility is for me to increase in wisdom and maturity, only then can I help my son and daughter.

- Don't remove the "ancient landmarks" as long as they still reflect God's intentions for us; prayerfully tear them down if they become a stumbling block to those who truly seek Him.

- A chauvinist male is to be pitied; he should be made to endure the careless attitudes and remarks that a so-called "contentious wife" has had to endure since Solomon was a pup.

- Riches are gotten with pain, kept with care, and lost with grief; the poor do not endure these embarrassments.

Perhaps you might like to compose a few proverbs of your own. Try your hand at it in your quiet time.

DAY 1

Proverbs 21:1–9

1 The king's heart is in the hand of the LORD, as the rivers of water: he turneth it whithersoever he will.

2 Every way of a man is right in his own eyes: but the LORD pondereth the hearts.

3 To do justice and judgment is more acceptable to the LORD than sacrifice.

4 An high look, and a proud heart, and the plowing of the wicked, is sin.

5 The thoughts of the diligent tend only to plenteousness; but of every one that is hasty only to want.

6 The getting of treasures by a lying tongue is a vanity tossed to and fro of them that seek death.

7 The robbery of the wicked shall destroy them; because they refuse to do judgment.

8 The way of man is froward and strange: but as for the pure, his work is right.

9 It is better to dwell in a corner of the housetop, than with a brawling woman in a wide house.

Reflecting on Proverbs 21:1–9

Meaning, please. . .

pondereth (21:2) weighs

high look (21:4) haughty eyes

plowing (21:4) lamp

Read and React
The cast list in these nine dramatic verses include the Lord, a king, a self-satisfied person, a haughty person, a diligent individual, a hasty person, a liar, a robber, a perverse person, and a brawling woman.

There's only one gender-specific role here—except for the Lord, though there are some who are trying to include Him, too.

We have met every one of these people earlier. We have seen them perform their roles three and four times before. It surely seems Solomon could have used a good editor. Why the repetition? First of all, as we have already agreed, these proverbs have come from a number of sources. Beyond that, these teachers are terribly concerned about specific issues; thus, they come up again and again. We will check out these nine statements and see if there is repetition here.

____ Verse 1: Somewhat of a new concept: The king's heart is in God's hand.

____ Verse 2: Not a new idea, but expressed differently: It's human nature for a person's ways to seem right to him, but God is the final judge.

____ Verse 3: The characters of justice, judgment, and sacrifice have appeared on this stage before. It is a truth worth repeating: All of the service and self-abasement in the world will not take the place of justice.

____ Verse 4: Self-importance is an anathema to the Lord. This has been expressed in at least a dozen previous settings. This is Solomon's gnawing concern.

____ Verse 5: A repeat: Hard work reaps a good harvest, while the rash can't claim the same.

____ Verse 6: The lying mouth, tongue, and lips have been a favorite theme. To use deception in order to gain riches is a deadly occupation.

____ Verse 7: Robbery stands for violence in this instance. Because they refuse to do what is just, they will be swept away.

____ Verse 8: There is nothing redeeming about the perverted man. But in contrast, the pure in heart are righteous. This is a very frequent issue in Proverbs. "Play it again, Solomon!"

___ Verse 9: And here it comes again. Women, brace yourselves! According to this teacher, it's better to be a "fiddler on the roof" than to endure an argumentative wife. Why this lame lambasting of women? "Tradition!"

Take Inventory
• William Cowper lived in the 1700s. He wrote:

> *Knowledge and wisdom, far from being one,*
> *Have oft times no connection. Knowledge dwells*
> *In heads replete with thoughts of other men:*
> *Wisdom in minds attentive to their own.*
> *Knowledge is proud that he has learn'd so much;*
> *Wisdom is humble that he knows no more.*

To Memorize
To do justice and judgment is more acceptable to the LORD than sacrifice. Proverbs 21:3

• • •

DAY 2

Proverbs 21:10–19
10 The soul of the wicked desireth evil: his neighbour findeth no favour in his eyes.

11 When the scorner is punished, the simple is made wise: and when the wise is instructed, he receiveth knowledge.

12 The righteous man wisely considereth the house of the wicked: but God overthroweth the wicked for their wickedness.

13 Whoso stoppeth his ears at the cry of the poor, he also shall cry himself, but shall not be heard.

14 A gift in secret pacifieth anger: and a reward in the bosom strong wrath.

15 It is joy to the just to do judgment: but destruction shall be to the workers of iniquity.

16 The man that wandereth out of the way of understanding shall remain in the congregation of the dead.

17 He that loveth pleasure shall be a poor man: he that loveth wine and oil shall not be rich.

18 The wicked shall be a ransom for the righteous, and the transgressor for the upright.

19 It is better to dwell in the wilderness, than with a contentious and an angry woman.

Reflecting on Proverbs 21:10–19

Meaning, please. . .

favour (21:10) mercy

reward in the bosom (21:14) hidden bribe

workers of iniquity (21:15) evildoers

Read and React

The theme of righteousness versus wickedness comes up for more discussion in this, the previous, and the next lessons. Before anyone blows the whistle and says, "Enough, already!" just remind yourself that humankind has wrestled with this theme since the third chapter of Genesis. And these BCers who are sacrificing animals to become righteous are still grappling with the tempting serpent, the illicit fruit, and the consequences of our first parents' disobedience.

The characteristics of wickedness are these:

___ Verse 10: They are without mercy. Consider the attributes of mercy—compassion to an offender.

___ Verse 11: They are scornful or contemptuous.

___ Verse 12: They are wicked, morally bad, evil.

___ Verse 13: They are compassionless, without pity or desire to assist.

___ Verse 14: They are dishonest, practice fraud or deception, and use underhanded practices.

___ Verse 15: They are workers of iniquity—they practice gross injustices.

___ Verse 16: They are backsliders. They have left the "straight and narrow" way.

___ Verse 18: They are transgressors—they violate God's commands.

___ Verse 19: They are contentious and of any gender! They exhibit an often perverse and wearisome tendency to quarrel.

Take Inventory
• The foregoing has dealt with the dark side of human experience—wickedness. Tomorrow's passage will give you an opportunity to discover the sunnier side of righteousness.

To Memorize
When the wise is instructed, he receiveth knowledge. Proverbs 21:11

• • •

Day 3

Proverbs 21:20–31
20 There is treasure to be desired and oil in the dwelling of the wise; but a foolish man spendeth it up.

21 He that followeth after righteousness and mercy findeth life, righteousness, and honour.

22 A wise man scaleth the city of the mighty, and casteth down the strength of the confidence thereof.

23 Whoso keepeth his mouth and his tongue keepeth his soul from troubles.

24 Proud and haughty scorner is his name, who dealeth in proud wrath.

25 The desire of the slothful killeth him; for his hands refuse to labour.

26 He coveteth greedily all the day long: but the righteous giveth and spareth not.

27 The sacrifice of the wicked is abomination: how much more, when he bringeth it with a wicked mind?

28 A false witness shall perish: but the man that heareth speaketh constantly.

29 A wicked man hardeneth his face: but as for the upright, he directeth his way.

30 There is no wisdom nor understanding nor counsel against the LORD.

31 The horse is prepared against the day of battle: but safety is of the LORD.

Reflecting on Proverbs 21:20–31

Meaning, please. . .

scaleth the city of the mighty (21:22) went up against a city of the mighty

strength of the confidence (21:22) stronghold of their confidence

keepeth (21:23) watch over

coveteth greedily (21:26) craves for more, covets

hardeneth his face (21:29) puts on a bold face

safety (21:31) victory

Read and React

In the last lesson, we concentrated on wickedness. In this selection, we will look for righteousness in the text. To be righteous is to put or be made right.

Let's look for the characteristics of those who are righteous in these twelve verses.

___ Verse 20: They are wise, or at least striving to obtain wisdom.

___ Verse 21: They are merciful—they think of others before themselves.

___ Verse 22: They are courageous; they seize opportunities to show the power of God.

___ Verse 23: They keep away from gossip and unsavory language. Remember Jesus' command in Psalm 19:14, "Let the words of my mouth. . .be acceptable in thy sight, O LORD, my strength, and my redeemer."

___ Verse 31: They are prepared—even their horses! Perhaps a major factor in godly maturity is preparation. If a horse is prepared against the battle, how much more must we be? Let's begin a list of Prep Points—you finish it.

Maturity Prep Points:

• Set up a daily quiet time when you will read the Bible. Pray about your day, and pray over your prayer list below.

• Begin a journal in which you will keep track of where you are in your walk in the Spirit. Include what you're reading, what you're praying about, your dreams and aspirations, and be sure to record answers to prayer!

• Select friends and loved ones you'd like to influence for Christ. Record their names in your journal. Pray for opportunities to influence them.

What can you add?

Take Inventory

- Righteousness is not an ominous word. There are those to whom it reflects what they call self-righteousness. But that's far from true. Remember, it means putting right. It is what the Lord is able to do in your heart and life. Consider starting your spiritual life journal. Don't become a slave to it, but allow your journal to be an intimate part of your growth in righteousness.

To Memorize

He that followeth after righteousness and mercy findeth life, righteousness, and honour. Proverbs 21:21

. . .

DAY 4

Proverbs 22:1–6

1 A good name is rather to be chosen than great riches, and loving favour rather than silver and gold.

2 The rich and poor meet together: the LORD is the maker of them all.

3 A prudent man foreseeth the evil, and hideth himself: but the simple pass on, and are punished.

4 By humility and the fear of the LORD are riches, and honour, and life.

5 Thorns and snares are in the way of the froward: he that doth keep his soul shall be far from them.

6 Train up a child in the way he should go: and when he is old, he will not depart from it.

Reflecting on Proverbs 22:1–6

loving favour (22:1) esteem

meet together (22:2) have this in common

Read and React

Wisdom and wealth are our topics in this selection. Often now, these sayings bring God into the equation, and by doing this, the writer is admitting that all promises of betterment are meaningless, unless God is included. As a matter of fact, they require God's involvement in order to come to pass in a human life. More specifically, we are entering a series of contrast parables—the wise ways versus foolish ways.

____ Verse 1: This is the first classic proverb in this group. It is a reminder that all names are fine, as long as the person who bears it carries with it a good reputation. To the sages of old, good repute was to be the most desired possession. Where would the tabloids be today if celebrities felt the same way?

____ Verse 2: Bringing the rich and the poor together was a major step for ancient writers. In this instance, Solomon is acknowledging that their common denominator is the Lord who created them. How should this then affect the relationship?

____ Verse 4: Perhaps number one on the list of the top ten concerns in Proverbs is the "fear of the LORD." In this verse it is praised for its consequences—"riches, honour, and life."

____ Verse 5: A paraphrase: "The wicked person's pathway is strewn with obstacles that cause pain by the soul's enemy; but he who is cautiously concerned for his soul is safe from them." Why? The Lord's involvement in "preventative medicine" cannot be overstated.

____ Verse 6: Parents who read this verse hold on to it for dear life. How many pastors have comforted the prodigal's mother with these words? How many dads try to believe it when a son or daughter angrily screeches out of the garage and down the street hell-bent for who knows what? All those years of morning and evening worship, Sunday school, church camp, Vacation Bible School, AWANA, teen group, evangelistic crusades, being a shepherd or an angel in the Christmas program, and taking cookies to shut-ins. Do those "train up a child in the way he should go"? Or is the real training an at-home industry: around the table, family prayers, shooting hoops in the driveway, talking about issues, goodnight hugs and kisses, goldfish funerals, discipline and punishment, and everything else that bespeaks love and caring?

Take Inventory

- How are you progressing in establishing a journal? Spend some time considering your own childhood and what you have learned from observation of your family. If you have children, put yourself in their shoes and evaluate your own home influences. If you have no children, how can you be an influential aunt, uncle, or even next-door neighbor to kids?

To Memorize

A good name is rather to be chosen than great riches. Proverbs 22:1

• • •

Day 5

Proverbs 22:7–13

7 The rich ruleth over the poor, and the borrower is servant to the lender.

8 He that soweth iniquity shall reap vanity: and the rod of his anger shall fail.

9 He that hath a bountiful eye shall be blessed; for he giveth of his bread to the poor.

10 Cast out the scorner, and contention shall go out; yea, strife and reproach shall cease.

11 He that loveth pureness of heart, for the grace of his lips the king shall be his friend.

12 The eyes of the LORD preserve knowledge, and he overthroweth the words of the transgressor.

13 The slothful man saith, There is a lion without, I shall be slain in the streets.

Reflecting on Proverbs 22:7–13

Meaning, please. . .

bountiful eye (22:9) generous

grace of lips (22:11) gracious speech

Read and React

This passage has seven verses dealing with matters that have become rather common in this study—rich, poor, money lenders, generosity, discipline, mockers, contention, purity, and laziness. But there's a slightly different twist on a couple of them.

___ Verse 8: "Sow. . .reap" is a familiar pairing in scripture, especially for proverbial sayings. In this case, sowing the seed and then harvesting or reaping the grain is the foundational fact that makes sowing wickedness and harvesting trouble identifiable to the farmers and migrant workers who heard this. The result? His ability to harm others will fail.

___ Verse 9: In these BC days, generosity was in short supply. Growing conditions were often poor, and poverty very nearly became a cottage industry. Beggars were as plentiful as locust. Have you ever been in a Third World country and bought a pack of Chiclets from a young salesman, only to have every little candy and gum seller in town sweep down upon you? Generosity can get you in trouble!

Still, here is the king urging generosity and telling his hearers that they shall be blessed if they follow this example. Generosity is described here as a "bountiful eye," which implies that mature people (those who should be generous) look for opportunities to share their bread with the poor. The promise? The Lord will bless.

___ Verse 10: If this proverb were written today, the teacher or preacher would probably say, "Tired of griping and complaining? Then clean house! Do one of two things: convert your mocking scorner, or get him out!" Sound drastic? The morale of any group can be totally shattered by mumblings from one malcontent. While it appears Solomon doesn't practice the three-strikes-and-your-out theory of discipline, it seems important to provide an opportunity for your agitator to get straightened out. If he won't, then, to quote Solomon, "Cast him out!"

___ Verse 13: The lazy sloth gets his just dues again. This time he attempts to excuse himself from work by reporting there is a lion outside, so he has no way to go work without risking life and limb. This excuse is so outlandish, the king himself must have had a smile on his face when he quoted it.

Many of us need to remind ourselves almost daily that maturity is the ability to see a job through, regardless of mood or the possibility of more interesting endeavors.

Take Inventory
• Of the four characters introduced above—the sower of wickedness, the practitioner of generosity, the malcontent, and the lazy excuse maker—which do you rub shoulders with in your daily life? One out of the four is a positive influence. What has been your technique for handling the other three?

To Memorize
The eyes of the LORD preserve knowledge, and he overthroweth the words of the transgressor. Proverbs 22:12

Day 6

Proverbs 22:14–21

14 The mouth of strange women is a deep pit: he that is abhorred of the LORD shall fall therein.

15 Foolishness is bound in the heart of a child; but the rod of correction shall drive it far from him.

16 He that oppresseth the poor to increase his riches, and he that giveth to the rich, shall surely come to want.

17 Bow down thine ear, and hear the words of the wise, and apply thine heart unto my knowledge.

18 For it is a pleasant thing if thou keep them within thee; they shall withal be fitted in thy lips.

19 That thy trust may be in the LORD, I have made known to thee this day, even to thee.

20 Have not I written to thee excellent things in counsels and knowledge,

21 That I might make thee know the certainty of the words of truth; that thou mightest answer the words of truth to them that send unto thee?

Reflecting on Proverbs 22:14–21

Meaning, please. . .

bow down thine ear (22:17) listen

fitted in thy lips (22:18) ready on your lips

Read and React

Here begin the five further collections of Proverbs. These are five separate collections of wisdom literature of various types. Of these five, first there is the collection of "Thirty Sayings of the Wise" (22:17–24:22).

In the eight verses of today's passage you will be reintroduced to some of the characters we have already been studying since 1:1.

____ Verse 14: The strange woman introduced here is more than an adulteress—she is the repository of all the dangers that women are capable of bringing to pass, in contrast to Lady Wisdom. Her description is very like the monster capable of swallowing alive all who come into its clutches. The ancients wrote about sea serpents with cavelike mouths that would attack ships and swallow the whole crew, ship and all. According to verse 14, this treatment is appropriate for all with whom the Lord is angry.

____ Verse 15: Here is the word *foolishness* again. At this point, folly is identified with a child's heart. This is a plea for discipline. It is not suggesting child abuse. To us, the word *rod* is frightening. But remember, this is figurative language. This is a plea for maturity. It's not an attempt to put old heads on young shoulders, but a reminder to guide your child into emotional as well as physical growth. Observant adults will read into this verse that there is a need for maturing regardless of your age.

____ Verses 17–19: For the first time, the theme of a proverb is expressed in three continuous verses. Paraphrased it reads: "Be wise and incline your ear to me and my words, for you will find it pleasant to keep them within your heart and mind. I have shared this with you today, so that your trust will be in the Lord."

____ Verses 20–21: The theme continues: "You can trust me. I have written these upcoming teaching proverbs as counsel and knowledge, so that I might impress upon you the certainty that the words are truth. Use these words to instruct and counsel."

The impact of these words in this second collection do bring a certainty to the reader that perhaps is missing in the previous chapters. You will continue to discover the impact of this collection.

Take Inventory
• Verse 17 raises the concept of "bowing down thine ear." Are you listening to God's wisdom?

To Memorize

Bow down thine ear, and hear the words of the wise, and apply thine heart unto my knowledge. Proverbs 22:17

. . .

DAY 7

Proverbs 22:22–29

22 Rob not the poor, because he is poor: neither oppress the afflicted in the gate:

23 For the LORD will plead their cause, and spoil the soul of those that spoiled them.

24 Make no friendship with an angry man; and with a furious man thou shalt not go:

25 Lest thou learn his ways, and get a snare to thy soul.

26 Be not thou one of them that strike hands, or of them that are sureties for debts.

27 If thou hast nothing to pay, why should he take away thy bed from under thee?

28 Remove not the ancient landmark, which thy fathers have set.

29 Seest thou a man diligent in his business? he shall stand before kings; he shall not stand before mean men.

Reflecting on Proverbs 22:22–29

Meaning, please. . .

spoil (22:23) despoil

strike hands (22:26) make pledges

sureties (22:26) guarantees

nothing to pay (22:27) no money to pay with

stand before kings (22:29) they will serve kings

Read and React

More from the "Thirty Sayings of the Wise." As you discovered in the previous selection, there is a difference between these proverbs and the others we have been working through for the past nine weeks. Many of these have elements of lectures or sermons. They burrow deeper into the meaning of the wise sayings, and the structure is more like the rest of scriptures, as opposed to isolated proverbs. The title comes from the fact that originally there were thirty chapters in an Egyptian manuscript by Amenemope that scholars believe this section of Proverbs is based upon. Its origins predate Solomon.

The *Teachings of Amenemope* was compiled to advise citizens who were involved in public service. The thirty sayings appear to be written with that audience in mind.

Striking sayings in this lesson's scripture follow:

____ Verses 22–23: The poor and the afflicted continue to be a principle topic in Proverbs. Previously, on the topics of poverty and the treatment of the handicapped, we were told to help the poor and be kind to them, but in this instance, we are confronted with an out-and-out command not to rob the poor or make life miserable for the afflicted. Today, the thought of robbing the poor is despicable, so is kicking the afflicted. But in that day, it was a natural occurrence. In Middle Eastern and Asian countries today, the people on the edge of society are treated with reverence, which is often a tenant of their religious faith.

If you do rob the poor, the Lord will become their attorney and plead their cause—and it's difficult to argue with that line of reasoning!

____ Verses 24–25: According to what we have learned about the "Thirty Sayings," association with a hot-tempered individual is off-limits, because you are liable to pick up his ways, which in turn endangers your soul. Little time should be spent with fools because there are too many others who need assistance. When seen in light of Amenemope the Egyptian's teachings, these pronouncements ring clear.

Take Inventory

- If you are not robbing the poor, is there any other kind of thievery you might be involved in? What about the theft of a person's good name and reputation? Or at least involvement in dropping hints of suspicion? What other kinds of robbery might good-hearted people like you be involved in?

To Memorize

Remove not the ancient landmark, which thy fathers have set. Proverbs 22:28

Week Ten

Proverbs 23 and 24

Now begins our tenth week in this study of Proverbs. It's too bad we can't have an up close and personal conversation with Solomon—kind of a "People Who Used to Be in the News" interview. If we could, it might sound like this.

MC: King Solomon, it's good to have you as our guest this evening.

Solomon: It is indeed a delight to be here.

MC: You and your influence have been around for quite a while. History books estimate that you and your father, King David, established the Israelite kingdom in 1000 BC. Correct?

Solomon: It has been such a long time ago, I do not remember the exact date! But that sounds about right.

MC: And you began construction on the Temple in Jerusalem sometime during the same century?

Solomon: In actuality, it was begun in the 480th year after my people came out of Egypt. That was the fourth year of my reign. I do recall that it was a huge undertaking, and it turned out pretty well, wouldn't you say?

MC: Actually, I've only seen artists' renderings. But, from what I've seen, it's most impressive.

Solomon: Yes, the Lord gave me wisdom to pull it off. You may read the details for yourself in what you have come to call the Holy Bible. I believe you would call the reference 1 Kings chapters 6 and 7. While you are at it, read my prayer in chapter 8. I wasn't too sure what to pray, but the Lord gave me wisdom.

MC: You have a way with words, King Solomon. Some of us have been studying the book of Proverbs. . .

Solomon: Oh yes, those.

MC: When did you find the time to write those thirty-one chapters?

Solomon: Well, young man, you must know that your chapter business is a modern tampering. We had no such arrangement in my day. Besides, as much as I would like to take credit for each and every word, I can't. Those wise sayings are the product of many minds. Many are mine, but I collected hundreds of others from many sources. I had a library full of them.

MC: Our time is up, Your Majesty, but I'd like to continue this conversation at another time. How long are you going to be in town?

Solomon: I think we could work something out. Have your secretary call my secretary and set something up.

DAY 1

Proverbs 23:1–9

1 When thou sittest to eat with a ruler, consider diligently what is before thee:

2 And put a knife to thy throat, if thou be a man given to appetite.

3 Be not desirous of his dainties: for they are deceitful meat.

4 Labour not to be rich: cease from thine own wisdom.

5 Wilt thou set thine eyes upon that which is not? for riches certainly make themselves wings; they fly away as an eagle toward heaven.

6 Eat thou not the bread of him that hath an evil eye, neither desire thou his dainty meats:

7 For as he thinketh in his heart, so is he: Eat and drink, saith he to thee; but his heart is not with thee.

8 The morsel which thou hast eaten shalt thou vomit up, and lose thy sweet words.

9 Speak not in the ears of a fool: for he will despise the wisdom of thy words.

Reflecting on Proverbs 23:1–9

Meaning, please. . .

what (23:1) or who

given to appetite (23:2) a big appetite

his dainties (23:3) food delicacies

labour not (23:4) don't wear yourself out

an evil eye (23:6) stingy man

Read and React

In a quick read of today's passage, there is a common topic running through these nine verses—food! As a matter of fact, eating was a favorite pastime in Holy Scripture, from a stolen fruit in the Garden of

Eden, to the Great Supper of the Lamb in Revelation.

Besides food, what is the other common denominator found in these verses? All but verse 9 have to do with a desire to be wealthy and influential. And most of it is written with a bit of humor.

____ Verse 1: Right from the top, we are introduced to the concept of putting on airs. The marginal reading of this verse substitutes the word *who* for *what*. In other words, be sure to notice who is at the table across from you or next to you. Your host, the ruler, just may have provided someone who can help you climb the ladder of success. Another interpretation is: Behave yourself; you don't know who's watching.

If you want to retain the "what" in this verse, our teacher is instructing his student to be observant—which fork to use, etc. That helps for getting ahead in the hoped-for "upper crust" of society.

____ Verse 2: Let's hope this verse was written with the teacher's tongue squarely in his cheek. Gluttony is the appropriate word here. The Greeks may have approved of voraciousness, but not this crowd. In refined circles, one eats slowly, taking small bites, and doesn't ask for seconds.

____ Verse 9: This verse and Jesus' instruction to not "cast ye your pearls before swine, lest they trample them under their feet, and turn again and rend you" (Matthew 7:6) appear to have a common lesson.

Take Inventory

• At your next dinner party, whether as host or guest, mentally test the lessons in this passage of scripture. As a matter of fact, test yourself, especially if you are with guests you don't know well. How do you conduct yourself? Acting like someone you're not is a strong temptation for many of us. Some other of Jesus' words are very appropriate here: "Seek ye first the kingdom of God, and his righteousness; and all these things shall be added unto you" (Matthew 6:33).

Seek ye first the kingdom of God, and his righteousness; and all these things shall be added unto you. Matthew 6:33

. . .

DAY 2

Proverbs 23:10–21

10 Remove not the old landmark; and enter not into the fields of the fatherless:

11 For their redeemer is mighty; he shall plead their cause with thee.

12 Apply thine heart unto instruction, and thine ears to the words of knowledge.

13 Withhold not correction from the child: for if thou beatest him with the rod, he shall not die.

14 Thou shalt beat him with the rod, and shalt deliver his soul from hell.

15 My son, if thine heart be wise, my heart shall rejoice, even mine.

16 Yea, my reins shall rejoice, when thy lips speak right things.

17 Let not thine heart envy sinners: but be thou in the fear of the Lord all the day long.

18 For surely there is an end; and thine expectation shall not be cut off.

19 Hear thou, my son, and be wise, and guide thine heart in the way.

20 Be not among winebibbers; among riotous eaters of flesh:

21 For the drunkard and the glutton shall come to poverty: and drowsiness shall clothe a man with rags.

Reflecting on Proverbs 23:10–21

Meaning, please. . .

old landmark (23:10) boundary stone

reins (23:16) innermost parts (soul)

an end (23:18) the future

expectation (23:18) hope

Read and React

___ Verse 10: Ancient or old landmarks are referred to in Proverbs more than once (22:28). Anyone who stole such stones to build a wall, make repairs, or to sell it was, in fact, stealing land and was a felon. With that in mind, look at the second half of the verse. The land in question was protected for widows and the fatherless. Oppressing them was an act strongly denounced.

___ Verse 11: The redeemer referred to is actually a relative of the persecuted and serves as a defender. Such defenders ferociously fought for their relatives' property. Something of this defender quality carried over into the New Testament as a characteristic of Jesus Christ.

___ Verses 13–14: Again, Proverbs focuses on disciplining children. To our twenty-first-century sensibilities, these words are unbearable, and we have heard them quoted by religionists who practice child abuse. Today, this extreme description of discipline may seem to verge on criminal acts. We are told in Deuteronomy that public stoning of rebellious children was allowed, but only as a parent's last resort (Deuteronomy 21:18–21). We shudder when we read those words, but some say such harsh treatment was necessary at this stage of Israel's development. Thank God for the coming of Jesus Christ!

___ Verse 15: "My boy, if your heart is wise, my heart will rejoice." Imagine a father holding a repentant child in his arms and blending tears of repentance and joy. That is my hope for all parents who read these words.

Take Inventory

• In your quiet time: If you are a parent, write a letter to one or all of your children. Let them know of the spiritual progress you are making.

Let them know that you are praying for each of them. Or, write to your parents and lovingly give them this good news. If you have neither parents nor children, write to a close friend. It is important that you share your faith.

Two Memorize

Apply thine heart unto instruction, and thine ears to the words of knowledge. Proverbs 23:12

. . .

DAY 3

Proverbs 23:22–26

22 Hearken unto thy father that begat thee, and despise not thy mother when she is old.

23 Buy the truth, and sell it not; also wisdom, and instruction, and understanding.

24 The father of the righteous shall greatly rejoice: and he that begetteth a wise child shall have joy of him.

25 Thy father and thy mother shall be glad, and she that bare thee shall rejoice.

26 My son, give me thine heart, and let thine eyes observe my ways.

Reflecting on Proverbs 23:22–26

Meaning, please. . .

hearken (23:22) listen

begat (23:22) sired; was father to

Read and React

These "Hearth and Home" proverbs are so different than those found in the first half of the book. Do you feel the gentleness? Even when speaking about coarse subjects, they are written more narratively and with understanding.

____ Verse 22: In this patriarchal society, the father becomes the lord of the home. All important instruction emanates from him. But of course, as a Proverbs reader, you have known that since chapter 1. There is a subtext here that is interesting. An enhanced paraphrase of this verse will bring it out:

"Listen to me, my children. As your father, I have every right to instruct you. And you have a God-ordained responsibility to hear, respond, and obey. Why? Because it was my seed that gave you life. Now I am telling you, do not hate your mother as she gets old. You will think she is treating you as a child, but she is still your mother. Her instructions continue to be true."

____ Verses 24–25: Before continuing this extended paraphrase, reread 10:1, 13:1, 15:20, and 19:13. Also look ahead to 28:7 and 29:3. "Any father and mother whose children have stayed true to father's teachings and mother's instructions is a righteous child. You are my righteous child, and I am rejoicing because of that fact. I have begotten wise children. And your mother, she who gave birth to you, rejoices! Praise the Lord!"

____ Verse 26: There was certainly an innate sense of child rearing psychology present in these pre–Dr. James Dobson days. (Child beating not included!) Just this week, a PhD in child development stated this same concept on *The Today Show.* That is, children who respect their parents will give them their love. Where does that respect come from? It's the day-by-day observations of the parents that kids are exposed to. They listen to the words that are expressed between them; they watch the so-called body language that reveals real intent; they observe and listen when parents are with other people.

It takes courageous and secure moms and dads to request their children to, " Observe us, and emulate our walk with God." Far too often it's, "Do as we say, and not as we do."

Take Inventory

To you readers who are not parents, take heart. What has been written applies to children of all ages. Aging parents are often in a most difficult situation. Most are too proud to confront their children at this stage of life, but inwardly they are crying for love and attention from their offspring. They are entrusting you with their hearts. There is that stage when child becomes parent to a parent. Most of us dread that time, but we who have been through it realize that it is a necessity and can be extremely rewarding for both.

To Memorize

Thy father and thy mother shall be glad, and she that bare thee shall rejoice. Proverbs 23:25

• • •

DAY 4

Proverbs 23:27–35

27 For a whore is a deep ditch; and a strange woman is a narrow pit.

28 She also lieth in wait as for a prey, and increaseth the transgressors among men.

29 Who hath woe? who hath sorrow? who hath contentions? who hath babbling? who hath wounds without cause? who hath redness of eyes?

30 They that tarry long at the wine; they that go to seek mixed wine.

31 Look not thou upon the wine when it is red, when it giveth his colour in the cup, when it moveth itself aright.

32 At the last it biteth like a serpent, and stingeth like an adder.

33 Thine eyes shall behold strange women, and thine heart shall utter perverse things.

34 Yea, thou shalt be as he that lieth down in the midst of the sea, or as he that lieth upon the top of a mast.

35 They have stricken me, shalt thou say, and I was not sick; they have beaten me, and I felt it not: when shall I awake? I will seek it yet again.

Reflecting on Proverbs 23:27–35

Meaning, please. . .

transgressors (23:28) unfaithful

moveth itself aright (23:31) goes down smoothly

heart (23:33) mind

Read and React

This is a temperance lesson for sure, or what most Christians understand to be abstinence. In this lesson, the proverb writer tosses a couple of social problems at the reader—prostitution and booze. We'll concentrate on the drinking issue because the strange woman topic has been considered frequently in Proverbs.

____ Verses 29–33: This is a rather forthright description of the harm liquor can do, starting with graphic descriptions of the mental and physical condition of those who hang around the bar too long. You can't miss these people; they are the ones with woes and sorrows, who'll argue at the drop of a hat, who babble on about nothing, who carry on their body wounds inflicted by falling and fighting, whose watery eyes are always bloodshot. They are the ones who will never be pictured in a liquor ad on the back cover of *Vanity Fair* magazine.

____ Verse 34: Mentally, the "winebibber" has frightening hallucinations that keep him off center and make him a laughing stock in the community. Even when he's sober, he has his highs (on a ship's mast) and lows (in the bottom of the sea).

___ Verse 35: There is a poignancy to this verse. The drunkard is beaten and slapped, but he cannot feel the punishment. It has been suggested that this is a picture of Israel. It, too, was kicked around, but God's people just kept on keeping on. Finally, the alcoholic acknowledges he is unable to control his habit, by admitting, "I will seek it yet again," which could be the start of rehabilitation.

Whatever the habit or thirst, it is vital to admit that we are a slave to it, that we have attempted all the tried-and-true methods of stopping, and that we are looking to find strength from outside ourselves. For believers, that strength is the Lord.

Take Inventory
• There are any number of intoxicants—those things that pull you away from what you know is God's will for you. They, too, cause sorrow and grief, and they cause your eyes to become red from weeping. It isn't just a down-and-out wino at the rescue mission who faces this kind of humiliation, it's up-and-outters, too, who have to admit their need and look to God.

• Share this idea with a friend. You might even need to keep it for yourself. This writer has been there. So have others. God offers His strength to you.

To Memorize
Hear thou, my son, and be wise, and guide thine heart in the way. Proverbs 23:19

Proverbs 24:1–12

1 Be not thou envious against evil men, neither desire to be with them.

2 For their heart studieth destruction, and their lips talk of mischief.

3 Through wisdom is an house builded; and by understanding it is established:

4 And by knowledge shall the chambers be filled with all precious and pleasant riches.

5 A wise man is strong; yea, a man of knowledge increaseth strength.

6 For by wise counsel thou shalt make thy war: and in multitude of counsellors there is safety.

7 Wisdom is too high for a fool: he openeth not his mouth in the gate.

8 He that deviseth to do evil shall be called a mischievous person.

9 The thought of foolishness is sin: and the scorner is an abomination to men.

10 If thou faint in the day of adversity, thy strength is small.

11 If thou forbear to deliver them that are drawn unto death, and those that are ready to be slain;

12 If thou sayest, Behold, we knew it not; doth not he that pondereth the heart consider it? and he that keepeth thy soul, doth not he know it? and shall not he render to every man according to his works?

Reflecting on Proverbs 24:1–12

Meaning, please. . .

heart studieth destruction (24:2) minds plot violence

thought (24:9) devising

Read and React

____ Verses 1–2: Here is advice to stay away from the wicked. They mean nothing but trouble. This same concept is also expressed in the sentiment of Proverbs 3:31 and Psalms 37 and 73. Have nothing to do with evil people!

_____ Verses 3–7: Back in 9:1, Lady Wisdom built her house. Now, another wise builder is hammering the first nails of his house. He has already settled the issues of site selection, building permits, architect's plans, etc. The wise builder has a thorough understanding of what's involved. Each room of his house will be pleasant and appropriate for the activities that will take place there. The wise builder will be successful because he is of strong mind and body.

_____ Verses 10–12: This trio of "If thou's" centers on an individual's capacity to be a mature child of God. "If you faint when trouble comes near, your strength is too small for the job." In the New Testament there are some good words for this situation; "Let us not be weary in well doing: for in due season we shall reap, if we faint not" (Galatians 6:9).

The next "If thou" is more difficult. This involves refusing to become involved in rescuing those who are being taken away for execution, even those who are stumbling to be slaughtered. It sounds as if this proverb is urging you to become (perish the thought) a radical! Commentators describe verse 11 as a plea to rescue those who are innocent, who have been wrongfully accused. Justice is a universal theme throughout the Old Testament.

Take Inventory

• Get involved in a justice ministry. First of all, ask the Lord to put a prayer project on your heart. Read your newspaper, watch news broadcasts, and peruse your national church publication for stories that relate to injustice. Contact government leaders and express your concerns. Become a passionate committee of one to talk up what's on your heart. Do what you do with a sense of humor. Write an op-ed piece or a letter to the editor for your newspaper. Support your church's overseas projects. Find out about a prison ministry in your town, or support one of the national programs. Get involved in justice.

To Memorize
A wise man is strong; yea, a man of knowledge increaseth strength.
Proverbs 24:5

. . .

Day 6

Proverbs 24:13–20

13 My son, eat thou honey, because it is good; and the honeycomb, which is sweet to thy taste:

14 So shall the knowledge of wisdom be unto thy soul: when thou hast found it, then there shall be a reward, and thy expectation shall not be cut off.

15 Lay not wait, O wicked man, against the dwelling of the righteous; spoil not his resting place:

16 For a just man falleth seven times, and riseth up again: but the wicked shall fall into mischief.

17 Rejoice not when thine enemy falleth, and let not thine heart be glad when he stumbleth:

18 Lest the LORD see it, and it displease him, and he turn away his wrath from him.

19 Fret not thyself because of evil men, neither be thou envious at the wicked;

20 For there shall be no reward to the evil man; the candle of the wicked shall be put out.

Reflecting on Proverbs 24:13–20

Meaning, please. . .

candle (24:20) lamp

Read and React

Is there anything stickier than honey? Some of us hate sticky fingers at breakfast. At the same time, there isn't much that is sweeter than honey. It is difficult to believe that anyone has to be told to eat honey.

____ Verses 13–14: With that lodged in our memory, the proverb writer turns us to knowledge and compares honey to his favorite subject—wisdom. In that BC day, honey was the great cure-all. Besides being sweet for bread and beverages, it supposedly had excellent medicinal properties. Like honey, wisdom is satisfying and sticks to your soul. When you find wisdom, you are rewarded, and your expectations are met.

____ Verses 15–16: Here begin a series of "Do nots." Of course they are written in somewhat reverse sentences. "Lay no wait," can be adequately rewritten to read, "Do not lie in wait like a highwaymen or bandits, in order to do violent acts to the righteous."

____ Verses 17–18: Do not rejoice when your enemy is brought down; don't let your heart rejoice even if he only stumbles a bit. Why? So that you will not displease the Lord with your rejoicing, and cause Him to turn His wrath from your enemy.

____ Verses 19–20: Do not fret over those who do evil, and that includes being envious of the wicked. The evil person gets no reward, and the wicked person's lamp is snuffed out.

St. Francis's Prayer

> *Lord, make me an instrument of Thy peace.*
> *Where there is hate, may I bring love;*
> *Where offense, may I bring pardon;*
> *May I bring union in place of discord;*
> *Truth, replacing error;*
> *Faith, where once there was doubt;*
> *Hope, for despair;*
> *Light, where there was darkness;*

Joy, to replace sadness.
Make me not so crave to be loved as to love.
Help me to learn that in giving I may receive;
In forgetting self, I may fine life eternal.

—St. Francis of Assisi

Take Inventory

- We all have heard a moving solo version of this prayer. It has been sung on numerous occasions. It always offers material for reflection. Take it with you into your quiet time. Reflect on peace, love, pardon, union, truth, faith, hope, light, joy, and life eternal.

To Memorize

Fret not thyself because of evil men. Proverbs 24:19

• • •

Day 7

Proverbs 24:21–34

21 My son, fear thou the LORD and the king: and meddle not with them that are given to change:

22 For their calamity shall rise suddenly; and who knoweth the ruin of them both?

23 These things also belong to the wise. It is not good to have respect of persons in judgment.

24 He that saith unto the wicked, Thou art righteous; him shall the people curse, nations shall abhor him:

25 But to them that rebuke him shall be delight, and a good blessing shall come upon them.

26 Every man shall kiss his lips that giveth a right answer.

27 Prepare thy work without, and make it fit for thyself in the field; and afterwards build thine house.

28 Be not a witness against thy neighbour without cause; and deceive not with thy lips.

29 Say not, I will do so to him as he hath done to me: I will render to the man according to his work.

30 I went by the field of the slothful, and by the vineyard of the man void of understanding;

31 And, lo, it was all grown over with thorns, and nettles had covered the face thereof, and the stone wall thereof was broken down.

32 Then I saw, and considered it well: I looked upon it, and received instruction.

33 Yet a little sleep, a little slumber, a little folding of the hands to sleep:

34 So shall thy poverty come as one that travelleth; and thy want as an armed man.

Reflecting on Proverbs 24:21–34

Meaning, please. . .

meddle (24:21) disobey

respect (24:23) partiality

one that travelleth (24:34) robber

want (24:34) poverty

Read and React
Further Sayings of the Wise:

____ Verse 23: *Respect* is the word selected in this version to mean "partiality." The first use of the word *respect* was in 1560, when its primary meaning was "to refrain from interfering with," as in, "God is no respecter of persons" (Acts 10:34). One can see how *respect* could mean our more contemporary word *partiality*.

____ Verses 24–26: Again, the theme of partiality has come to the fore. It is not God's plan that the wicked shall be called righteous or innocent of wrongdoing—that is showing partiality, and in this case, it is an abhorrence. The wicked are to be rebuked and shown the sinfulness of their ways. To one who rebukes, a good blessing will come his way. And to such a one, those honest words are like a kiss on the lips.

___ Verse 27: The need for a good work ethic and planning is ever with us. Again, a proverb writer broaches ill planning and laziness, this time in a positive way. "Get your outside work done, then think about building a new house." Plan carefully—step by step. Acquire your money before tackling a major job.

___ Verses 30–34: These five verses make up the longest single proverb in the book. And as you may expect, it's about the idler. He is unreliable, unfulfilled, beset by problems, hungry, full of excuses, never finishes a job, poverty-stricken, and incorrigible.

Take Inventory
- "My son, fear thou the LORD and the king" (24:21). Give some thought to this verse during your quiet time. It is agreed that *fear* is to "respect" or "honor." If you have children in your home, what is being said that encourages such respect for God? Sometime when you are watching television, have your family count the number of times the phrase "Oh my God!" is exclaimed. Do you think it's using the Lord's name in vain?

To Memorize
My son, fear thou the LORD and the king. Proverbs 24:21

WEEK ELEVEN

PROVERBS 25, 26, AND 27

"These are also proverbs of Solomon, which the men of Hezekiah king of Judah copied out" (Proverbs 25:1).

King Hezekiah reigned 715–687 BC. He was twenty-five years old when he assumed the throne of Judah from his father Ahaz. You will remember it was a divided kingdom during this period. While Hezekiah was king of Judah, Hoshea was on the throne in Israel.

These were bright days for Judah, as Hezekiah followed in the footsteps of his ancestor King David. He removed cultic worship objects like Moses' bronze serpent on a pole, which was used in rituals to prevent or cure snake bites. His religious reforms were recognized and highly praised. Not since King David had there been the singing of hymns in worship. Hezekiah restored that practice. His interests in the words of David prompt scholars to believe that the king encouraged the compilation of Solomon's proverbs.

A Page from Contemporary Life

It is really quite obvious that we are back in a collection of Solomon's proverbs. He still doesn't have anything good to say about fools and sloths.

I was called a lazy sloth once. The summer after my high school graduation, in order to get some more money together for college, I went on a job search for a position that paid well and that wouldn't upset my schedule too much. My dad accused me of being a dilettante in my looking. He said I had to decide to take any job in order to make some real money. Then he added the dilettante stuff: "Or you can stay out the first semester, so you can keep up with your summer social life."

It was pretty plain that dad's sarcastic suggestion wasn't an option, so I recombed the *Tribune* want ads until I found the position that had me standing in line at a time clock at 7:00 a.m. in the Del Monte cannery with a brand-new Teamsters card in my wallet. That's also when I met Alonzo, my summer boss.

My job, so Alonzo told me, was to eject cans of freshly cooked apricots out of a pigeon-holed frame into the cardboard box I had just folded and slapped up on the front of the machine. Those cans of apricots came careening down a spiral shoot from the cooker upstairs and into my machine. If I wasn't fast enough, the cans would pile up and start cascading down on me and my fellow Teamster workers. This is when Alonzo entered the picture with expletives that can't be printed.

"Miller, why are you so lazy?" he'd bark from across the way. "Whatta ya doin'? Standin' around thinkin' highfalutin college boy thoughts?" Then he'd yell, "You're a lazy bum, that's what you are."

"I'm not lazy, Alonzo, I just don't have the hang of it yet."

Then his face would become a deeper red, and he'd holler, "If you're not a lazy bum, then you're a fool! Even a girl can run this machine!" While he yelled, he'd kick the equipment, and I felt every bit the lazy fool he made me out to be. That went on all summer. Cannery work was not my cup of apricot juice.

Earlier we said that proverbs usually used hyperbole to get their point across—so do I. Now, let's see what's awaiting us this week.

Day 1

Proverbs 25:1–15

1 These are also proverbs of Solomon, which the men of Hezekiah king of Judah copied out.

2 It is the glory of God to conceal a thing: but the honour of kings is to search out a matter.

3 The heaven for height, and the earth for depth, and the heart of kings is unsearchable.

4 Take away the dross from the silver, and there shall come forth a vessel for the finer.

5 Take away the wicked from before the king, and his throne shall be established in righteousness.

6 Put not forth thyself in the presence of the king, and stand not in the place of great men:

7 For better it is that it be said unto thee, Come up hither; than that thou shouldest be put lower in the presence of the prince whom thine eyes have seen.

8 Go not forth hastily to strive, lest thou know not what to do in the end thereof, when thy neighbour hath put thee to shame.

9 Debate thy cause with thy neighbour himself; and discover not a secret to another:

10 Lest he that heareth it put thee to shame, and thine infamy turn not away.

11 A word fitly spoken is like apples of gold in pictures of silver.

12 As an earring of gold, and an ornament of fine gold, so is a wise reprover upon an obedient ear.

13 As the cold of snow in the time of harvest, so is a faithful messenger to them that send him: for he refresheth the soul of his masters.

14 Whoso boasteth himself of a false gift is like clouds and wind without rain.

15 By long forbearing is a prince persuaded, and a soft tongue breaketh the bone.

Reflecting on Proverbs 25:1–15

Meaning, please. . .

discover (25:9) disclose

infamy (25:10) ill repute

a wise reprover upon an obedient ear (25:12)
a wise rebuke to a listening ear

Read and React

There are wonderful metaphors and similes in the early part of this collection. An English translation cannot do justice to the wit and word pictures.

____ Verse 1: This constitutes the introduction to this collection. Commentators mention the fact that the earlier "Thirty Sayings" collection was from Egypt. Now this Hezekiah-produced collection is from Judah, a country which had close contact with Egypt. Teachers of Hezekiah's day were strong proponents of human wisdom, but like the earlier chapters, they warn that God cannot be left out of the account.

____ Verses 2–7: It is a given that since this collection originated in the court of King Hezekiah, the issue of kingship would appear right off the bat.

____ Verses 11–12: Gold and silver (see 17:3) represent elements that have withstood testing in order to make them malleable for the jeweler to work with. A paraphrase of these verses: "A word spoken appropriately, at the right time and with sincerity, is like a golden apple sitting on a setting of silver," and an "earring or ornament of gold is like the wise words of correction, lovingly delivered to the ear of a righteous person."

____ Verses 14–15: The power of well-chosen words is of concern to the king here. He worries about promises that are not fulfilled, like rain clouds that don't produce showers.

Take Inventory
• Well-chosen words aren't what they used to be; hurried-off e-mail has taken care of that. Consider your words. How are they perceived? Do others always understand what you really mean, or are you judged by your tone of voice? One of the most welcome ministries today is delivered by the postman—a genuine note or letter. You've taken time to send the very best.

To Memorize
A word fitly spoken is like apples of gold in pictures of silver. Proverbs 25:11

. . .

DAY 2

Proverbs 25:16–23
16 Hast thou found honey? eat so much as is sufficient for thee, lest thou be filled therewith, and vomit it.

17 Withdraw thy foot from thy neighbour's house; lest he be weary of thee, and so hate thee.

18 A man that beareth false witness against his neighbour is a maul, and a sword, and a sharp arrow.

19 Confidence in an unfaithful man in time of trouble is like a broken tooth, and a foot out of joint.

20 As he that taketh away a garment in cold weather, and as vinegar upon nitre, so is he that singeth songs to an heavy heart.

21 If thine enemy be hungry, give him bread to eat; and if he be thirsty, give him water to drink:

22 For thou shalt heap coals of fire upon his head, and the LORD shall reward thee.

23 The north wind driveth away rain: so doth an angry countenance a backbiting tongue.

Reflecting on Proverbs 25:16–23

Meaning, please. . .

withdraw thy foot (25:17) be seldom in your neighbor's house

maul (25:18) a war club

nitre (25:20) a wound

Read and React

Today's selection has outdone itself in colorful language. Among the verbal treasures are themes that are everyday in content. As has been said previously, this collection is written with more verve and drama, with an eye to attracting attention. These are surely indications of King Hezekiah's courtly influence.

The following is a study of the very human and down-to-earth themes found in these eight verses:

___ Verse 16: Previously, the honey metaphor was thought of as a means to sweetly get a point across or to lubricate a difficult situation. The use of honey in this instance is strictly as a delicious food that one is able to get too much of with disastrous results. Perhaps the overriding lesson is discipline. How does this apply to you?

___ Verse 17: Withdrawing your foot is a folksy way to say, "Don't overstay your welcome." How does this apply to you?

___ Verse 18: Lying about your neighbor, whether in court or a block party, is improper for a maturing child of God. It's as deadly as using implements of war on him or her or them! How does this apply to you?

___ Verse 19: To rely on an unfaithful person when you need help is as comforting as the maladies mentioned: a sore tooth or a lame foot. They're not too reliable, are they? How does this apply to you?

___ Verse 20: There is no use trying to cheer up a person with a heavy heart. Don't bother singing jolly songs. It hurts as much as cold weather or antiseptic on an open wound. So what do you do instead?

___ Verses 21–22: If you really want to annoy your enemy, be kind to him; give him food and drink. It will be like building a fire on his head. The Lord will reward your kindness. How does this apply to you?

___ Verse 23: Want to drive away rain (or just about anything else)? Keep your mean-looking countenance and backstabbing tongue. Hmm. . .what do you think?

Take Inventory
• These proverbs get kind of personal. Here is your opportunity to talk to yourself. Spend some quiet time responding to these proverb interpretations.

To Memorize
If thine enemy be hungry, give him bread to eat; and if he be thirsty, give him water to drink. Proverbs 25:21

• • •

DAY 3

Proverbs 25:24–26:6
24 It is better to dwell in the corner of the housetop, than with a brawling woman and in a wide house.

25 As cold waters to a thirsty soul, so is good news from a far country.

26 A righteous man falling down before the wicked is as a troubled fountain, and a corrupt spring.

27 It is not good to eat much honey: so for men to search their own glory is not glory.

28 He that hath no rule over his own spirit is like a city that is broken down, and without walls.

Proverbs 26

1 As snow in summer, and as rain in harvest, so honour is not seemly for a fool.

2 As the bird by wandering, as the swallow by flying, so the curse causeless shall not come.

3 A whip for the horse, a bridle for the ass, and a rod for the fool's back.

4 Answer not a fool according to his folly, lest thou also be like unto him.

5 Answer a fool according to his folly, lest he be wise in his own conceit.

6 He that sendeth a message by the hand of a fool cutteth off the feet, and drinketh damage.

Reflecting on Proverbs 25:24–26:6

Meaning, please. . .

troubled, corrupt (25:26) polluted, muddied

glory (26:27) honor

curse causeless (26:2) undeserved curse

Read and React

Let's continue where we left off yesterday. We have more personal proverbs ahead of us. Be ready to respond.

____ Verse 24: This again! Suffice to say again, it must have been the inspiration for the musical *Fiddler on the Roof.* You have to admit, it's a humorous concept! How does it apply to you?

____ Verse 25: In time of war and chaos, "good news from a far country" is as welcome as the cold water mentioned here. Is there any truth to the saying "No news is good news"?

____ Verse 26: Why would any righteous person "fall down" before the wicked? "Fall down" can be interpreted as "gives in" or "gives way." Solomon says that righteous person is as beneficial as muddied and polluted water. How in our twenty-first-century world do we cave in to wickedness?

____ Verse 27: More honey! Try this interpretation: "Seeking for one honor after another is like overdoing your consumption of honey." It's too much of a good thing. It will take its toll on your ego, just as honey does with your stomach. How does this apply to you?

____ Verse 28: This proverb is very straightforward. Its point is discipline and self-control. Need more be said? In what areas does the Lord need to help your self-control?

Chapter 26 contains fool proverbs that need little comment:

____ Verse 1: Fools need many things, but according to the proverb, honor is not one of them. It's about as beneficial as snow in summer and rain at harvest.

____ Verse 4: "The silly questions of a fool do not have to be answered. If you do, you may be thought of as a fool yourself."

____ Verse 5: "Don't attempt to reason with a fool, or you'll look like one yourself."

____ Verse 6: "Don't entrust a fool with delivering any messages for you. You'll just be stabbing yourself in the foot."

Who decides when a fool is a fool? Are there individuals in your life who have been dismissed as fools, but you know if they were treated with patience, love, and understanding, they could make a contribution?

Take Inventory
• Work these parables through in your quiet time. Prayerfully consider the final paragraph above.

To Memorize
As cold waters to a thirsty soul, so is good news from a far country. Proverbs 25:25

• • •

Day 4

Proverbs 26:7–17
7 The legs of the lame are not equal: so is a parable in the mouth of fools.

8 As he that bindeth a stone in a sling, so is he that giveth honour to a fool.

9 As a thorn goeth up into the hand of a drunkard, so is a parable in the mouth of fools.

10 The great God that formed all things both rewardeth the fool, and rewardeth transgressors.

11 As a dog returneth to his vomit, so a fool returneth to his folly.

12 Seest thou a man wise in his own conceit? there is more hope of a fool than of him.

13 The slothful man saith, There is a lion in the way; a lion is in the streets.

14 As the door turneth upon his hinges, so doth the slothful upon his bed.

15 The slothful hideth his hand in his bosom; it grieveth him to bring it again to his mouth.

16 The sluggard is wiser in his own conceit than seven men that can render a reason.

17 He that passeth by, and meddleth with strife belonging not to him, is like one that taketh a dog by the ears.

Reflecting on Proverbs 26:7–17

Meaning, please. . .

parable (26:7) proverb

bindeth (26:8) tying

thorn (26:9) thornbush

own conceit (26:12) his own eyes

his bosom (26:15) the dish

render a reason (26:16) answer discreetly

Read and React

Do you remember the "therefore" concept in geometry? Well, most of these verses need a "therefore" sign. Nearly all of them complete in themselves, and every verse ends with a period. But the reader is often left in the air, as some are like cliffhangers. The moral is not always included. But here is something to remember: When the BC folks read or heard these metaphors and similes, they knew exactly what Solomon had in mind. These proverbs are couched in the social ways of that day. They were everyday events and happenings.

____ Verse 7: Therefore, the fool is unable to understand the full meaning of a parable. Your interpretation: _____

_____

____ Verse 8: No fool who ties a stone in a sling has any hope of the stone leaving the sling and hitting its target; therefore, it is foolhardy to honor him. Your interpretation: _____

_____

____ Verse 9: Therefore, both fools and drunkards do as much harm to others, as well as themselves, trying to speak a parable or slinging a thornbush around. Your interpretation: _____

_____

____ Verse 12: Therefore, self-centered people are bigger losers than fools. Your interpretation: _____

_____

____ Verse 16: Therefore, it has to be said, the self-centered sluggard is so stuffed with his own importance, he's tried to outdo seven men who know what they're doing. Your interpretation: _____

_____

There is nothing too profound in this lesson. In fact, this has been a tribute to Solomon and Hezekiah's senses of humor.

Taking Inventory

• You may want to reread these parables and then write a few of your own. You might use one of Solomon's as your model. Write a parody. In place of fools and sluggards, write yours to reflect your job, home, school, or whatever.

• As a writer I might write one like this: "As a writer has to return to his manuscript, as tired as he may be of it, he knows it's the Lord's assignment. Sometimes it might be more fun to be foolish, but that won't make my publisher happy."

To Memorize

Now therefore hearken unto me, O ye children: for blessed are they that keep my ways. Proverbs 8:32

Day 5

Proverbs 26:18–28

18 As a mad man who casteth firebrands, arrows, and death,

19 So is the man that deceiveth his neighbour, and saith, Am not I in sport?

20 Where no wood is, there the fire goeth out: so where there is no talebearer, the strife ceaseth.

21 As coals are to burning coals, and wood to fire; so is a contentious man to kindle strife.

22 The words of a talebearer are as wounds, and they go down into the innermost parts of the belly.

23 Burning lips and a wicked heart are like a potsherd covered with silver dross.

24 He that hateth dissembleth with his lips, and layeth up deceit within him;

25 When he speaketh fair, believe him not: for there are seven abominations in his heart.

26 Whose hatred is covered by deceit, his wickedness shall be shewed before the wholecongregation.

27 Whoso diggeth a pit shall fall therein: and he that rolleth a stone, it will return upon him.

28 A lying tongue hateth those that are afflicted by it; and a flattering mouth worketh ruin.

Reflecting on Proverbs 26:18–28

Meaning, please. . .

in sport (26:19) only joking

dissembleth with his lips (26:24) covers real self through talking

Read and React

The fool comes into his own in this chapter. Folly isn't spelled out in so many words, but it is entertainingly illustrated. One critic says that fools knows all about wisdom and can even get involved in "wisdomy" sounding conversations. He knows all about proverbs, but isn't quite sure what to do with them. Some of us remember our student days when we had a brain full of information but didn't know what to do with it. Fortunately, we eventually figured it out. But not the fool!

A fool is not necessarily a clown. He's not one of Shakespeare's comic relief characters. No, the fool of Proverbs can be smart as a whip, well-mannered, and know how to eat an artichoke.

So why are fools always the example of how not to be? Read today's passage and observe the verbal cartoons of the lazy people or fools that are sketched out there. Do their incredible excuses sound familiar? Maybe not their exact words, but the so-called reasoning behind them.

First of all, fools are not going to learn from reading about themselves, but hopefully, those striving to be mature will learn from their mistakes. It's been said before that Solomon, or whoever, almost always uses exaggeration or hyperbole to make the point. A fool will only take these vignettes at face value, but the spiritually alert will catch the point.

There are also some remarks in this passage about how to destroy friendships. The foolish are experts at this.

____ Verses 18–28: These sounds like a scene from the Fourth of July, with a foolish neighbor shooting off bottle rockets and then telling his neighbor, "Sorry that landed on your roof, you know I'm just having fun."

Then there is the gossip in verse 20 who visits the other neighbors with the bottle rocket story and has embroidered it so much that those who were present that night wouldn't even recognize what really happened!

And in verse 28, "I had nothing to do with that bottle rocket," lies the perpetrator. "Why, the Jones's are my best friends in the cul-de-sac."

Foolish people don't always make the best friends.

Take Inventory

- The weekly shopper paper carries a much-read advice column. Last week's column had a sniveling young man bemoaning that his friends were a bad influence on him, but he didn't want to drop them. If he did, he'd have no friends. How would you have responded to him?

To Memorize

The words of a talebearer are as wounds, and they go down into the innermost parts of the belly. Proverbs 26:22

· · ·

DAY 6

Proverbs 27:1–13

1 Boast not thyself of to morrow; for thou knowest not what a day may bring forth.

2 Let another man praise thee, and not thine own mouth; a stranger, and not thine own lips.

3 A stone is heavy, and the sand weighty; but a fool's wrath is heavier than them both.

4 Wrath is cruel, and anger is outrageous; but who is able to stand before envy?

5 Open rebuke is better than secret love.

6 Faithful are the wounds of a friend; but the kisses of an enemy are deceitful.

7 The full soul loatheth an honeycomb; but to the hungry soul every bitter thing is sweet.

8 As a bird that wandereth from her nest, so is a man that wandereth from his place.

9 Ointment and perfume rejoice the heart: so doth the sweetness of a man's friend by hearty counsel.

10 Thine own friend, and thy father's friend, forsake not; neither go into thy brother's house in the day of thy calamity: for better is a

neighbour near than a brother far off.

11 My son, be wise, and make my heart glad, that I may answer him that reproacheth me.

12 A prudent man foreseeth the evil, and hideth himself; but the simple pass on, and are punished.

13 Take his garment that is surety for a stranger, and take a pledge of him for a strange woman.

Reflecting on Proverbs 27:1–13

Meaning, please. . .

faithful are the wounds (27:6) well-meant wounds

full soul (27:7) full person

calamity (27:10) problems

Read and React

Relationship is still the theme of today's passage. Again it is expressed in individual sayings. Solomon was unbelievably aware of what was transpiring between the people under his rule. For a king, he had a genuine grasp of human nature.

____ Verses 1–2: Here is a warning about bragging or boasting. The Hebrew word for *praise* is the same as for *boast*. That makes sense. You can boast about someone else, and that's called praise. But when you toot your own horn, that most certainly is boasting.

____ Verse 4: This verse is a question that demands an answer. Envy is jealousy, and jealousy is what Shakespeare calls "the green-eyed monster"—the creature that fills its captives with hate and rage and even murder. Oh foolish man, foolish woman, let God's Holy Spirit take control of your emotions.

On a more positive note, this passage goes on to speak of the joy and fun of friendship. Fortunate is the person who has friends to laugh and eat with. Think of all that friendship offers.

___ Verse 9: Isn't a friend's hearty counsel sweet? It is said that women rely more on that kind of relationship than men do. But, male reader, thank God for a male friend who will listen and empathize.

___ Verse 10: When calamity strikes, "better is a neighbor near than a brother far off." Every one of us has a story we could share.

Does a king have friends? Was Solomon ever lonely? He probably had scores of professional friends around him. What did these sayings mean to him?

Take Inventory
• An anonymous poem carved into a Scottish church pew.

> *If after kirk ye bide a wee,*
> *There's some would like to speak to ye;*
> *If after kirk ye rise and flee,*
> *We'll all seem cold and stiff to ye.*
> *The one that's in the seat wi' ye,*
> *Is stranger here than you, may be;*
> *All here hae got their fears and cares—*
> *Add you your soul unto our prayers;*
> *Be you our angel unawares.*

• Meditate upon this sentiment in your quiet time.

To Memorize
Thine own friend, and thy father's friend, forsake not. Proverbs 27:10

Day 7

Proverbs 27:14–27

14 He that blesseth his friend with a loud voice, rising early in the morning, it shall be counted a curse to him.

15 A continual dropping in a very rainy day and a contentious woman are alike.

16 Whosoever hideth her hideth the wind, and the ointment of his right hand, which bewrayeth itself.

17 Iron sharpeneth iron; so a man sharpeneth the countenance of his friend.

18. Whoso keepeth the fig tree shall eat the fruit thereof: so he that waiteth on his master shall be honoured.

19 As in water face answereth to face, so the heart of man to man.

20 Hell and destruction are never full; so the eyes of man are never satisfied.

21 As the fining pot for silver, and the furnace for gold; so is a man to his praise.

22 Though thou shouldest bray a fool in a mortar among wheat with a pestle, yet will not his foolishness depart from him.

23 Be thou diligent to know the state of thy flocks, and look well to thy herds.

24 For riches are not for ever: and doth the crown endure to every generation?

25 The hay appeareth, and the tender grass sheweth itself, and herbs of the mountains are gathered.

26 The lambs are for thy clothing, and the goats are the price of the field.

27 And thou shalt have goats' milk enough for thy food, for the food of thy household, and for the maintenance for thy maidens.

Reflecting on Proverbs 27:14–27

Meaning, please. . .

dropping (27:15) rain dripping

hideth her (27:16) restraining her

countenance (27:17) wits

waiteth (27:18) takes care of

answereth to face (27:19) reflects a face

bray (27:22) crush

Read and React

The friends, the contentious woman, an iron man, a couple of fruit venders, the metal smiths, the guy with the loud voice—they're all here. And all of them have a lesson to teach us. Read on for more illustration of some of these lessons:

____ Verse 14: The king is still attempting to teach us to get along with each other. In my imagination of this proverb, a young man is so excited that he has gained the friendship of the neighborhood cutie, he can't keep quiet about it. But he embarrasses her with his loud proclamations of love and loses her.

The secret of a good friendship is to recognize the feelings of the other person. One can be overly enthusiastic and demonstrative over a friend. Play it warmly cool!

____ Verse 15: Rumor has it that the Smiths over on Elm Street are having problems. To be gender protective, let's just say it's not just rain showers that are dripping! There's a moody mate who's driving the neighborhood crazy with his/her sniffing around and outpouring of the other mate's lesser qualities.

____ Verse 18: Luigi is a prizewinning fig grower. He doesn't own the orchard, but he works for its generous owner, who says, "Yes, this is my fig farm, and Luigi is my prized employee. He may eat as many figs as he wishes and may take them home to his family. I trust him, and he does good work for me."

In Jesus' parable a rancher told his hired hand, "Thou hast been faithful over a few things, I will make thee ruler over many things" (Matthew 25:21).

___ Verses 23–27: It is remarkable the way God provides for His people. We meet a sheep and goat rancher in these verses who might have said, "When we inherited this property, it was so rundown that the livestock had little to graze and were dying. Today, thanks to the Lord, we are clothed in lambs wool, and we sell goats' milk to the co-op."

God does reward faithfulness.

Take Inventory
- Faithfulness in small things—isn't that the secret of success? You, on the path of spiritual maturity, will discover this. Have you made your discovery yet?

To Memorize
Be thou diligent to know the state of thy flocks, and look well to thy herds. Proverbs 27:23

WEEK TWELVE
PROVERBS 28 AND 29

The rather uncreative title for these two chapters in the Authorized King James Version is "More Proverbs." If I were a newspaper journalist and were asked to write an overriding headline to chapters 28 and 29, I might try something like: "A Gallery of Human Foibles and Divine Enablements" or "Out of a King's Wise Imaginings and Heart" or "Finding the 'I' in Maturity."

A Page from Contemporary Life

MC: Welcome back to the show. We are indeed privileged to have His Royal Majesty, Solomon, King of Israel, son of David, and of course, author of that best-selling volume on spiritual maturity, *Proverbs*.

Solomon: Thank you for your cordial welcome. It makes me think of what I wrote in what you call chapter 29 in my proverb book, "Many seek the ruler's favour; but every man's judgment cometh from the LORD." Verse 26, I believe.

MC: I don't understand.

Solomon: Oh really? You are not a sluggard, are you?

MC: No, I don't think so, but why did that particular proverb come to mind?

Solomon: All the applause and whistling made me think of the long lines of favor seekers who lined up outside my audience hall. They made such a show of currying my favor.

MC: So?

Solomon: What most of them needed was not their neighbor's land, but justice. I couldn't provide the kind they needed.

MC: Why not?

Solomon: Because a ruler or a lawyer can only care for temporal matters. Most people need justice for their souls. That comes from the Lord.

MC: Any other words of knowledge from you?

Solomon: Do you think anyone in Washington knows about me?

MC: Thinking about running for office?

Solomon: Oh my, no, I don't think my way of ruling would be acceptable. You know, I'm not democratic.

MC: Is that with a lowercase *d*? Anything else you'd like to say, Your Majesty?

Solomon: Yes, now that you mention it. I wrote quite an appropriate proverb for you: Do you want someone who is hasty in speech? There is more hope for a fool than for anyone like that. Chapter 29, verse 20.

Day 1

Proverbs 28:1–8

1 The wicked flee when no man pursueth: but the righteous are bold as a lion.

2 For the transgression of a land many are the princes thereof: but by a man of understanding and knowledge the state thereof shall be prolonged.

3 A poor man that oppresseth the poor is like a sweeping rain which leaveth no food.

4 They that forsake the law praise the wicked: but such as keep the law contend with them.

5 Evil men understand not judgment: but they that seek the LORD understand all things.

6 Better is the poor that walketh in his uprightness, than he that is perverse in his ways, though he be rich.

7 Whoso keepeth the law is a wise son: but he that is a companion of riotous men shameth his father.

8 He that by usury and unjust gain increaseth his substance, he shall gather it for him that will pity the poor.

Reflecting on Proverbs 28:1–8

Meaning, Please. . .

transgression of a land (28:2) when there is rebellion

usury (28:8) exorbitant interest on a loan

Read and React

While the Solomon interview is "creative history," it raises an interesting issue: How would Solomon be accepted inside the Beltway today? Forget political parties and current administrations, would Solomon, King of Israel, have a hearing in Washington?

Within the confines of these two chapters, we'll investigate the king's interests in what seem to be today's world's interests, starting with 28:1–8 and ahead to 28:9–16 and even a few verses from 28:17–24.

Social issues	Church and state	Poverty
28:13	28:1	28:3
28:15	28:5	28:5
28:16	28:10	28:6
		28:8
		28:11

Health care	Natural resources	National defense
28:15	28:15	28:2
	28:19	28:17

Homeland security	Justice Department.
28:4	28:8
28:7	28:9
28:12	
28:17	

That covers some verses in this assignment and the next couple. We're not taking it any further than this. You might enjoy continuing this exercise through chapter 29. There are some factors you ought to think about while reading each day's scripture portion:

1. Is this a problem today, or is it primarily a BC situation?

2. Find a contemporary translation, and discover new meanings to these verses, and perhaps assign them to different classifications.

3. How would the White House and/or Congress respond?

4. If you wish to change or add to any of the assigned references, feel free to do so.

Take Inventory
• Complete the assignment above.

To Memorize
Whoso keepeth the law is a wise son. Proverbs 28:7

. . .

DAY 2

Proverbs 28:9–16

9 He that turneth away his ear from hearing the law, even his prayer shall be abomination.

10 Whoso causeth the righteous to go astray in an evil way, he shall fall himself into his own pit: but the upright shall have good things in possession.

11 The rich man is wise in his own conceit; but the poor that hath understanding searcheth him out.

12 When righteous men do rejoice, there is great glory: but when the wicked rise, a man is hidden.

13 He that covereth his sins shall not prosper: but whoso confesseth and forsaketh them shall have mercy.

14 Happy is the man that feareth alway: but he that hardeneth his heart shall fall into mischief.

15 As a roaring lion, and a ranging bear; so is a wicked ruler over the poor people.

16 The prince that wanteth understanding is also a great oppressor: but he that hateth covetousness shall prolong his days.

Reflecting on Proverbs 28:9–16

Meaning, please. . .

turneth away his ear (28:9) turn a deaf ear

rise (28:12) rise to power

a man is hidden (28:12) go into hiding

wanteth understanding (28:16) lacks understanding

covetousness (28:16) ill-gotten gain

Read and React

If they had BC lawyers back in Solomon's day, some of their ways of thinking rubbed off on him. Legal situations raise the litigation heads in today's scripture.

___ Verse 9: There's not much hope for anyone who turns a deaf ear to the law. But is that religious law, or the law of the land? Good question. They are both the same. In fact, the lawyers of Solomon's day were the Pharisees.

___ Verse 10: It's a binding promise that has as much authority as the legal court—whoever causes the righteous to go astray in an evil way shall fall himself into his own pit. Some believe this pit refers to official stoning.

___ Verse 11: The rich man had a hugely inflated estimate of himself, and he also had the law on his side. He was probably a big contributor. To be seen in his company meant a boost to one's image. But there was a downside—his riches too often came illegally. Pharisees learned to turn blind eyes or deaf ears to what was transpiring—thus the stigma on the name *Pharisee*.

___ Verse 13: Here is the sinner who attempts to hide his underhandedness. If the payment was just right, he could get a friendly Pharisee lawyer to help him cover over the traces of his illegal act. Solomon says such a man will not prosper. He might temporarily, but not in eternity.

___ Verses 15–16: Now Solomon looks squarely at his own kind, those whom the long arm of the law can't reach—rulers and kings and potentates. When Solomon's father, David, took another man's wife as his own, it took God's prophet Nathan to confront him with his sin.

If a ruler wants to behave like an animal toward his beaten-down people, he will be called wicked. But, if he wants the understanding and love of his people, he will have to stop being the oppressor and give up his ill-gotten treasures.

Take Inventory

• Aspiring to spiritual maturity demands constant work. Remember when someone you loved told you, "If it's worth doing at all, it's worth doing well."

As I write, I am praying for you. And as King Solomon would say, "Be thou diligent!" (Proverbs 27:23).

To Memorize

The upright shall have good things. Proverbs 28:10

• • •

DAY 3

Proverbs 28:17–24

17 A man that doeth violence to the blood of any person shall flee to the pit; let no man stay him.

18 Whoso walketh uprightly shall be saved: but he that is perverse in his ways shall fall at once.

19 He that tilleth his land shall have plenty of bread: but he that followeth after vain persons shall have poverty enough.

20 A faithful man shall abound with blessings: but he that maketh haste to be rich shall not be innocent.

21 To have respect of persons is not good: for for a piece of bread that man will transgress.

22 He that hasteth to be rich hath an evil eye, and considereth not that poverty shall come upon him.

23 He that rebuketh a man afterwards shall find more favour than

he that flattereth with the tongue.

24 Whoso robbeth his father or his mother, and saith, It is no transgression; the same is the companion of a destroyer.

Reflecting on Proverbs 28:17–24

Meaning, please. . .

stay him (28:17) offer him assistance

vain persons (28:19) worthless pursuits

respect (28:21) partiality

Read and React

The topic here is prosperity—a subject for which there are no short-cuts or guaranteed schemes. Hard work is the key to prosperity. Solomon finds no fault with honest labor that results in success—even the success of finally making ends meet. It's the selfish, self-centered operator who compromises to see riches. Such a person is blind, fool-ish, and his actions are futile.

According to Solomon, the key to success depends on one thing—one's trust in God. People who trust in themselves instead of the Lord are as equally stupid as those who give no thought for tomorrow.

___ Verse 19: Everyone wants to make an easy buck. Talk to farmers of any era; there is nothing easy about tilling the ground, milling and grinding grain, or providing the bread and other fixings to feed a farm family and the crew. If there is a lucky fix of some sort, no real farmer has found it yet. His prosperity depends on the sweat of his brow.

___ Verse 20: There have always been folks who take off after some worthless pursuit or another. According to Proverbs, those folks will have "poverty enough," but the "faithful man shall abound with blessing."

Take Inventory

• Though none are particularly spiritual, think about the following quotations from some well-known people:

"Few of us can stand prosperity. Another man's I mean."

MARK TWAIN

"Prosperity can only be lasting if it is based on justice."

THEODORE ROOSEVELT

"The virtue of Prosperity is temperance; the virtue of Adversity is fortitude."

FRANCIS BACON

"Prosperity proves the fortunate; adversity, the great."

PLINY THE YOUNGER

"Why is Jesus so quiet about good prosperity and Christianity?"

ANONYMOUS

To Memorize

A faithful man shall abound with blessings. Proverbs 28:20

DAY 4

Proverbs 28:25–28

25 He that is of a proud heart stirreth up strife: but he that putteth his trust in the LORD shall be made fat.

26 He that trusteth in his own heart is a fool: but whoso walketh wisely, he shall be delivered.

27 He that giveth unto the poor shall not lack: but he that hideth his eyes shall have many a curse.

28 When the wicked rise, men hide themselves: but when they perish, the righteous increase.

Reflecting on Proverbs 28:25–28

Meaning, please. . .

proud heart (28:25) greedy

hideth his eyes (28:27) turns a blind eye

Read and React

Our schedule being what it is, this session is limited to four verses. The poor and wicked are still with us, on paper at any rate. The common word in the first two verses is *heart*, but not one modern English translation retains the word *heart*.

____ Verse 25: "He that is of a proud heart stirreth up strife." At face value, this phrase appears to be a simple observation that folks who are proud and haughty make trouble for everybody else.

In contemporary English, *proud heart* means "greedy person," which gives the lesson a whole new slant. According to Bible dictionaries, greed is one of the most basic sins. It is one of the classic "Cardinal Sins," as well as another example of self-centeredness—the seeming blight of our civilization, as well Solomon's.

____ Verse 26: It's a common expression, "I know my own heart." Now we read in Proverbs that if we trust in our hearts, we are fools. Two out of three modern translations substitute the word *wits* for heart, which makes sense. So now we read, "If we trust our own wits, we are pretty foolish." I don't know about your wits, but mine let me down on occasion!

The other half of this verse reads, "but whoso walketh wisely, he shall be delivered." Is there some kind of corollary between the two halves of this verse? If we don't live by our wits, but walk wisely (in the Lord), we will be delivered. Delivered?

Like a loaf of bread? Delivered from what? Most modern Bible translations drop *delivered* and use the promise, "We will come through safely."

A simple summary of this verse: "Trust in the Lord and walk in wisdom."

____ Verse 27: This is being written while volunteers for the Salvation Army are collecting contributions in the malls. It is so amusing to watch people avert their eyes (or "hideth their eyes") when they walk by one of the bell ringers. Even when they are greeted with a "Merry Christmas!" they are unable to look the kettle keeper in the eye.

Solomon was writing of a different situation, but there is certainly a commonality here. The reward for these eye averters? "They shall have many a curse!"

Take Inventory
• "Trust in the Lord and walk in wisdom." Can we be expected to do anything less? In your quiet time, spend some moments considering those words. Write them on a plaque, or better yet, on your heart.

To Memorize
He that giveth unto the poor shall not lack. Proverbs 28:27

Day 5

Proverbs 29:1–9

1 He, that being often reproved hardeneth his neck, shall suddenly be destroyed, and that without remedy.

2 When the righteous are in authority, the people rejoice: but when the wicked beareth rule, the people mourn.

3 Whoso loveth wisdom rejoiceth his father: but he that keepeth company with harlots spendeth his substance.

4 The king by judgment establisheth the land: but he that receiveth gifts overthroweth it.

5 A man that flattereth his neighbour spreadeth a net for his feet.

6 In the transgression of an evil man there is a snare: but the righteous doth sing and rejoice.

7 The righteous considereth the cause of the poor: but the wicked regardeth not to know it.

8 Scornful men bring a city into a snare: but wise men turn away wrath.

9 If a wise man contendeth with a foolish man, whether he rage or laugh, there is no rest.

Reflecting on Proverbs 29:1–9

Meaning, please. . .

establisheth the land (29:4) gives stability

overthroweth land (29:4) ruins the land

Read and React

Power and righteousness can be strange bedfellows, but in Proverbs, power is tempered by the godly impact of righteousness. Here again we are focusing in on the nature and fruit of both righteousness and its flipside—wickedness. As Solomon has done throughout these chapters, we will look once again at the way righteousness and wickedness affect our homes and community. It is in society's best interest that righteousness instead of wickedness flourishes.

____ Verse 4: First of all, it is necessary for rulers to rule with godly justice that will keep the country stable and their reign stable. A paraphrase of verse 4 might read, "It is by instilling justice that a king is able to bring stability to his land, but it can still be ruined by citizens who demand too much." Is there any correlation between this and our own country?

____ Verse 6: It is the duty of righteous citizens to "let their lights shine!" Sometimes the only way that can be done is by rejoicing out loud. The evil man needs to be drowned out.

____ Verse 7: Righteous leadership must make provisions for the poor. Taking the King James Version text at face value, we read "the cause of the poor." Perhaps it is not too far off track to interpret that to mean "what is causing poverty in our country."

____ Verses 8–9: The influence of high and mighty know-it-alls on the community will probably bring increased tension in place of hoped-for and much-needed harmony, and that is another reason to elect righteous people to serve elected offices. "If a wise man contendeth with a foolish man, whether in rage or laughter, there is no rest."

____ Verse 1: Now, back to a ring leader in disharmony. This person is often corrected and warned about his attitude, but there is no change. Instead he becomes more belligerent, his blood pressure rises, he has a stroke, and he dies. Why? Because wickedness has possessed him. What responsibility did the righteous have toward this damaged person?

Take Inventory

• Today's lesson is important. It is amazing to read how Solomon and the others gave such close attention to community. In your quiet time, consider your involvement.

To Memorize

The righteous considereth the cause of the poor. Proverbs 29:7

. . .

Day 6

Proverbs 29:10–18

10 The bloodthirsty hate the upright: but the just seek his soul.

11 A fool uttereth all his mind: but a wise man keepeth it in till afterwards.

12 If a ruler hearken to lies, all his servants are wicked.

13 The poor and the deceitful man meet together: the LORD lighteneth both their eyes.

14 The king that faithfully judgeth the poor, his throne shall be established for ever.

15 The rod and reproof give wisdom: but a child left to himself bringeth his mother to shame.

16 When the wicked are multiplied, transgression increaseth: but the righteous shall see their fall.

17 Correct thy son, and he shall give thee rest; yea, he shall give delight unto thy soul.

18 Where there is no vision, the people perish: but he that keepeth the law, happy is he.

Reflecting on Proverbs 29:10–18

Meaning, please. . .

uttereth all his mind (29:11) gives full vent to anger

faithfully judgeth the poor (29:14) judges poor with equity

Read and React

The topics of power and righteousness are continued. Wickedness in high places became a rallying cry for the righteous. Punishments varied. You will remember that when it became public knowledge that King David had taken the married Bathsheba for himself, the Lord forbade him to build the temple. That assignment went to Solomon, the son of David and Bathsheba.

The forty-year reign of King Solomon over Israel became polluted with his indiscretions and acceptance of the gods of other nations. In 1 Kings 11:1–3, "King Solomon loved many strange women, together with the daughter of Pharaoh, women of the Moabites, Ammonites, Edomites, Zidonians, and Hittites. . . . He had seven hundred wives, princesses, and three hundred concubines."

It is said that when Solomon was old, his wives turned his heart to other gods, which meant his heart was not perfect with the Lord his God, as was the heart of David his father. God caused enemies to war against Israel and Solomon. Finally "Solomon slept with his fathers, and was buried in the city of David his father: and Rehoboam his son reigned in his stead" (1 Kings 11:43).

____ Verse 17: Nothing is said of Solomon's son Rehoboam in any of the wisdom books. Some feel this verse and many others in the collection could be a description of the king's relationship to his own son. Discipline was very high on Solomon's list of parental duties. Because of the boy's age, the father knew he was a natural to assume the throne—the BC Prince William.

____ Verse 18: This is one of the highlight verses in all of Proverbs: "Where there is no vision, the people perish." In modern translation, the word *vision* has been replaced with "revelation" or "prophecy." A paraphrase: "Where there is no hope for the future, no revelation of what is on the horizon, people will throw off their restraint. There will be chaos and mutiny."

For believers everywhere, this verse needs to be written over every pulpit and altar and breakfast table and front door. The clergy, the laity, and their families need to be committed to these words.

Take Inventory

- What is your vision for yourself and your family? In what way can you help yourself find that vision? How can such a vision be impressed on the minds and hearts of our families? Use your quiet time to work this through.

To Memorize

Where there is no vision, the people perish: but he that keepeth the law, happy is he. Proverbs 29:18

• • •

Day 7

Proverbs 29:19–27

19 A servant will not be corrected by words: for though he understand he will not answer.

20 Seest thou a man that is hasty in his words? there is more hope of a fool than of him.

21 He that delicately bringeth up his servant from a child shall have him become his son at the length.

22 An angry man stirreth up strife, and a furious man aboundeth in transgression.

23 A man's pride shall bring him low: but honour shall uphold the humble in spirit.

24 Whoso is partner with a thief hateth his own soul: he heareth cursing, and bewrayeth it not.

25 The fear of man bringeth a snare: but whoso putteth his trust in the LORD shall be safe.

26 Many seek the ruler's favour; but every man's judgment cometh from the LORD.

27 An unjust man is an abomination to the just: and he that is upright in the way is abomination to the wicked.

Reflecting on Proverbs 29:19–27

Meaning, please. . .

delicately bringeth up (29:21) pamper

bewrayeth it not (29:24) discloses nothing

Read and React

____ Verse 19: In a royal palace, or a rich person's estate, servants appear to be the most difficult problem that royalty and the moneyed have to endure. In this instance, the servant is uncontrollable. Evidently, physical discipline is all he will respond to. One critic suggests he really understands but is too stiff-necked to obey. Is this another reason to used "the rod"?

____ Verse 20: Speaking in haste can be a difficult situation for anyone—those moments when you wish you could reach out and grab your words before they reach the other person's ears and brain. If this is a problem for you, our proverb writer adds insult to injury by saying, "There is more hope for a fool than for him."

____ Verse 21: Evidently slave owners often raised children from infancy. The advice in the proverb suggests that you don't want to pamper this child you are raising because the young person will probably come to a bad end.

____ Verse 22: An individual who is given to anger is capable of stirring up strife, and a hot head causes all sorts of problems. Does this strike any responsive chord in you?

____ Verse 23: As you would expect, a person's pride shall bring him or her humiliation, but the humble in spirit will be honored.

____ Verse 24: At this point it seems Solomon's collection of Proverbs is getting a little low. Nonetheless, here is one about thieving: If you're a thief's partner, you'll probably hate your job, and even when you hear a victim cursing and calling out, you keep your mouth shut in fear.

___ Verse 25: Some people are fearful about getting caught in a trap, but if your trust the Lord, you'll be safe.

___ Verse 26: Only a king could share this. There are people who go out of their way to court the king's favor, but in reality, they should be more concerned about the Lord, who will judge them in the last day.

___ Verse 27: Evidently, everybody is an abomination to someone. This final Solomon proverb can be paraphrased like this: "The unjust person is an abomination to the righteous, but the upright are an abomination to the wicked." So, whose abomination are you?

Take Inventory
• If you are not using the discussion questions above, you would do well to consider these three during your quiet time. The trust and obey coupling is interesting. Should help in some radical soul searching.

To Memorize
Honour shall uphold the humble in spirit. Proverbs 29:23

WEEK THIRTEEN
PROVERBS 30 AND 31

So begins our last week in Proverbs. As promised, we are moving away from "More of Solomon's Proverbs," and into "The Sayings of Agur." Your guess as to who this Agur is, is as good as anyone else's. According to 30:1, he was the son of Jakeh. Some modern translations have designated Agur an oracle. We will deal with this authorship issue briefly in our first day of study. The style and content of chapter 30 is different from what we have experienced in the first twenty-nine chapters. This is going to be an interesting final week together.

A Page from Contemporary Life

On Saturday, August 24, 1996, my son Tim, and daughter-in-law Donna, flew out of the Seattle airport for Bucharest and their first term as missionaries in Romania. Since I was unable to be present for the Seattle send-off, we'd said our good-byes earlier, and I used their departure time as what Dag Hammarskjold called a "marking" moment.

Could I ever forget that certain Sunday evening service when Tim was a little boy? I remember the event as if it had happened yesterday. We were settling in the family pew, coats draped over the back, crayons ready, and not just a few "shhhhs." That's when Lisa noticed her brother wasn't sitting with us.

"How come Tim gets to sit with friends and not with us?"

I glanced over at her mother. "He's with the children's choir in the balcony."

"Oh," was her succinct answer. "Just wait until I'm his age," she mumbled.

The speaker of the evening was a missionary. His message was aimed at the young—to dedicate their lives for possible missionary service. At the close of his stirring address, we stood and sang some verses of "A Charge to Keep I Have." The earnest speaker was making an appeal for young people to come forward, but no one made a move.

In anticipation of getting home for a snack and a little television, I was gathering up coats and coloring stuff when Lisa tugged at me, "Look, Daddy. . ."

And there was Tim, almost all the way down the aisle and starting for the long altar rail. He was alone. He dropped to his knees and buried his blond head. Our son was making a commitment to God's will—whatever it be. I went up and knelt beside him. My heart was proud and heavy at the same time, but then I passed it off with, "Lord, let's get him out of grade school before we sweat China."

Some twenty-seven years later, it wasn't China—it was Romania. To me, this is what the family issues in Proverbs are all about.

Day 1

Proverbs 30:1–9

1 The words of Agur the son of Jakeh, even the prophecy: the man spake unto Ithiel, even unto Ithiel and Ucal,

2 Surely I am more brutish than any man, and have not the understanding of a man.

3 I neither learned wisdom, nor have the knowledge of the holy.

4 Who hath ascended up into heaven, or descended? who hath gathered the wind in his fists? who hath bound the waters in a garment? who hath established all the ends of the earth? what is his name, and what is his son's name, if thou canst tell?

5 Every word of God is pure: he is a shield unto them that put their trust in him.

6 Add thou not unto his words, lest he reprove thee, and thou be found a liar.

7 Two things have I required of thee; deny me them not before I die:

8 Remove far from me vanity and lies: give me neither poverty nor riches; feed me with food convenient for me:

9 Lest I be full, and deny thee, and say, Who is the Lord? or lest I be poor, and steal, and take the name of my God in vain.

Reflecting on Proverbs 30:1–9

Meaning, please. . .

Agur, Jakeh, Ithiel, Ucal (30:1) names of unknown personages

brutish (30:2) too stupid

pure (30:5) proves true

Read and React

Nothing is known of Agur, Jakeh, Ithiel, or Ucal. They may well be of foreign origin. In other words, there is a mystery that hangs over this chapter, not unlike the mystery that centers on Agur's confession.

____ Verses 2–3: Agur's confession: "I am brutish, too stupid, have no human understanding, have not learned wisdom, and have no knowledge of God." Then to make his point that he doesn't know the Holy One, he asks questions about Him. Some scholars feel that these negatives about himself are Agur's personal irony. Perhaps the ancient world was aware that the man was anything but like these statements. Self-effacement has often been a personality trait in the Middle East.

____ Verse 4: Agur's questions about the Almighty indicate he was not totally ignorant about God. Some think this is a series of riddles looking for the answer "God."

____ Verse 5: In the very next verse, Agur tells his readers, "Every word of God can be proven true." He continues with the assurance, "He is a protecting shield to every person who put his or her trust in Him." And Agur does not know the Holy One?

And he continues with a warning:

____ Verse 6: "Do not add anything to His words, or else He will rebuke you!" Do paraphrases count?

____ Verses 7–9: In this pious prayer, Agur requests to be kept from falsehood and dishonesty and to be kept from great wealth and poverty.

This is going to be an interesting week of study!

Take Inventory

• If Agur's words that he is ignorant about the things of God are true, how would you lead him to an understanding of the Lord in very simple terms? Write a letter to Agur in your quiet time.

To Memorize

Every word of God is pure: he is a shield unto them that put their trust in him. Proverbs 30:5

Day 2

Proverbs 30:10–19

10 Accuse not a servant unto his master, lest he curse thee, and thou be found guilty.

11 There is a generation that curseth their father, and doth not bless their mother.

12 There is a generation that are pure in their own eyes, and yet is not washed from their filthiness.

13 There is a generation, O how lofty are their eyes! and their eyelids are lifted up.

14 There is a generation, whose teeth are as swords, and their jaw teeth as knives, to devour the poor from off the earth, and the needy from among men.

15 The horseleach hath two daughters, crying, Give, give. There are three things that are never satisfied, yea, four things say not, It is enough:

16 The grave; and the barren womb; the earth that is not filled with water; and the fire that saith not, It is enough.

17 The eye that mocketh at his father, and despiseth to obey his mother, the ravens of the valley shall pick it out, and the young eagles shall eat it.

18 There be three things which are too wonderful for me, yea, four which I know not:

19 The way of an eagle in the air; the way of a serpent upon a rock; the way of a ship in the midst of the sea; and the way of a man with a maid.

Reflecting on Proverbs 30:10–19

Meaning, please. . .

horseleach (30:15) Hebrew meaning uncertain. It may be a leech used for medicinal purposes.

Read and React

Again we trespass into Agur's domain, where imagery is strange and discomforting. Awaiting us are ravenous ravens that are ready to peck out our eyeballs so young eagles can eat them. Welcome to the mysterious world of Agur, son of Jaketh.

____ Verses 10–17: One teacher has called this block of scripture Agur's argument for cautious assertiveness. And so he gives one of his picturesque illustrations—cursing a person, and not just swearing at him, but casting a spell on him or something similar. Servants were thought to "cast spells" over their masters and disgruntled children over parents and their inheritances. Keep your nose out of other people's business, says Agur.

Agur compares the selfish "gimmee" instinct in the human race with the suction of bloodletting leeches (verse 15)—another example of the writer's daring imagery. Often over the top, one could say for near certain that his convictions and passions were to the level of twenty-first-century radicals and rabble-rousing demonstrators. He let the chips fall as they may; he seems to have had nothing to lose.

____ Verses 18–19: Here are four delightfully poetic lines. First Agur tells the reader that there are three things that are almost too wonderful for him to think about, maybe even four. And they are the way an eagle soars in the air, the movement of a serpent upon a rock, the motion and balance of a ship in the sea, and the way of a man with a maid. Don't ask for a meaning of these four lines; just enjoy them. I have learned something from reconsidering Agur: First impressions are not always good or correct. Who would have thought?

Taking Inventory

How would you interpret verse 19?

To Memorize

Remove far from me vanity and lies. Proverbs 30:8

Day 3

Proverbs 30:20–31

20 Such is the way of an adulterous woman; she eateth, and wipeth her mouth, and saith, I have done no wickedness.

21 For three things the earth is disquieted, and for four which it cannot bear:

22 For a servant when he reigneth; and a fool when he is filled with meat;

23 For an odious woman when she is married; and an handmaid that is heir to her mistress.

24 There be four things which are little upon the earth, but they are exceeding wise:

25 The ants are a people not strong, yet they prepare their meat in the summer;

26 The conies are but a feeble folk, yet make they their houses in the rocks;

27 The locusts have no king, yet go they forth all of them by bands;

28 The spider taketh hold with her hands, and is in kings' palaces.

29 There be three things which go well, yea, four are comely in going:

30 A lion which is strongest among beasts, and turneth not away for any;

31 A greyhound; an he goat also; and a king, against whom there is no rising up.

Reflecting on Proverbs 30:20–31

Meaning, please. . .

odious (30:23) unloved

conies (30:26) rock badgers

comely (30:29) stately

Read and React

Open the great book of Agur proverbs—or riddles—and today you will discover more startling images and equally jarring prose, but nothing as beautiful as yesterday's four lines. If a modern editor were working on Mr. Agur's manuscript, I believe he would have separated verses 18 and 19 from verse 20. It's really quite jarring!

___ Verses 21–23: And here we are, back to itemizing three and four categories of Agur's reaction to life around him. Here are four things the earth cannot bear:

A servant who becomes king
A fool who has stuffed himself with food
An unloved woman who is married
And a maidservant who displaces her mistress

It really is a little strange that someone could be so upset by these four happening that his world trembles. Agur must have been terribly sensitive.

___ Verses 24–28: And now, it's four little creatures who are cunning:

The ants prepare for winter.
The badgers live comfortably in stone crags.
Locusts seem well organized without a king.
Lizards (not spiders) can be caught with a hand, but are even in the king's palace.

___ Verses 29–31: There are three things that move in stride, and a fourth that is stately:

A lion, which is the strongest and bravest beast
A strutting rooster (not the KJV greyhound)
A he–goat
And a king!

There you have it. The cream of Agur's crop.

Take Inventory
• Read and think.

> *O Word of God incarnate,*
> *O Wisdom from on high,*
> *O Truth unchanged, unchanging,*
> *O Light of our dark sky,*
> *We praise Thee for the radiance*
> *That from the hallowed page,*
> *A lantern to our footsteps,*
> *Shines on from age to age.*

—WILLIAM WALSHAM HOW

To Memorize
Whoso walketh uprightly shall be saved. Proverbs 28:18

• • •

Day 4

Proverbs 30:32–31:9
32 If thou hast done foolishly in lifting up thyself, or if thou hast thought evil, lay thine hand upon thy mouth.

33 Surely the churning of milk bringeth forth butter, and the wringing of the nose bringeth forth blood: so the forcing of wrath bringeth forth strife.

Proverbs 31
1 The words of king Lemuel, the prophecy that his mother taught him.

2 What, my son? and what, the son of my womb? and what, the son of my vows?

3 Give not thy strength unto women, nor thy ways to that which destroyeth kings.

4 It is not for kings, O Lemuel, it is not for kings to drink wine; nor for princes strong drink:

5 Lest they drink, and forget the law, and pervert the judgment of any of the afflicted.

6 Give strong drink unto him that is ready to perish, and wine unto those that be of heavy hearts.

7 Let him drink, and forget his poverty, and remember his misery no more.

8 Open thy mouth for the dumb in the cause of all such as are appointed to destruction.

9 Open thy mouth, judge righteously, and plead the cause of the poor and needy.

Reflecting on Proverbs 30:32–31:9

Meaning, please. . .

lifting up thyself (30:32) exalted yourself

lay thine hands upon thy mouth (30:32) clap your hands over your mouth

wringing of the nose (30:33) twisting of the nose

King Lemuel (31:1) next proverb writer/collector

Read and React

Finally, here are Mr. Agur's final proverbs. Two very practical, down-to-earth pieces of advice that involve keeping your mouth shut and the engagement of troublemaking.

___ Verse 32: So you've made a fool of yourself. But who hasn't? According to Agur, if you can't keep quiet, "lay thine hand upon thy mouth."

___ Verse 33: Cause and effect is a legitimate way of looking at actions. It goes without saying: If you stir up ire and anger, you're going to have a fight on your hands. It's as simple as day and night.

Thank you, Agur. We have enjoyed your occasional flashes of brilliance, your humor, the truth you shared with us—and those four magnificent lines of poetry.

• • •

And now in the center ring is our final collector of noble phrases and pithy remarks,

King Lemuel and his thirty-one verses, which include the favorite Mother's Day sermon text of all times.

But first, who is King Lemuel? Good question. Like Agur, we have no idea who he is, or if in fact, he was a king. It's quite certain that he was never king over the Israelites.

___ Verses 1: This is the introduction. A direct explanation that Lemuel is a prophetic oracle, who learned his trade from his mother.

___ Verses 2–7: As per Solomon's teachings, the mother is to be the child's teacher and advice giver. Her advice to young Lemuel is presented in three exhortations:

• Avoid other women. We will be careful not to read to much into that request.

• Remember her vows to God made at the time of his birth.

• Remember his royal obligation to the oppressed.

___ Verses 8–9: Finally, his clear call to royal responsibility: Speak up for those who are unable to speak for themselves, and judge fairly.

To the teachings of such a man, we are dedicating the final three lessons in this book.

Take Inventory
• If you are a parent, what kind of expectations have you spelled out to

your children? If you're not a parent, how were you aware of your parents expectations for you?

To Memorize
Open thy mouth, judge righteously, and plead the cause of the poor and needy. Proverbs 31:9

. . .

Day 5

Proverbs 31:10–16
10 Who can find a virtuous woman? for her price is far above rubies.

11 The heart of her husband doth safely trust in her, so that he shall have no need of spoil.

12 She will do him good and not evil all the days of her life.

13 She seeketh wool, and flax, and worketh willingly with her hands.

14 She is like the merchants' ships; she bringeth her food from afar.

15 She riseth also while it is yet night, and giveth meat to her household, and a portion to her maidens.

16 She considereth a field, and buyeth it: with the fruit of her hands she planteth a vineyard.

Reflecting on Proverbs 31:10–16

Meaning, please. . .

virtuous woman (31:10) a wife of noble character

no need of spoil (31:11) lacks nothing of value

maidens (31:15) serving girls

Read and React

We shall spend the last days of our study discovering the "The Wife of Noble Character." It really makes no difference who King Lemuel is—he has left us a literary gem, recognized by everyone. In its King James form printed here, the reader is asked, "Who can find a virtuous woman?" For centuries the word *virtuous* did not have the overtones it has today. Virtue has something to do with virginity, which was not what Old Testament writers wanted it limited to.

____ Verse 10: And we begin! Modern scholars and critics have begun to use the title, "The Complete Woman," for verses 10–31. Others have titled this section, "The Truly Capable Woman."

The fact that Lemuel's sayings came from his mother certainly suggests that the writing of this paean to womanhood was influenced by her. The twenty-two verses comprise an acrostic, each line beginning with a different letter of the twenty-two-letter Hebrew alphabet. This was a popular poetry form. Because of this, the sequence of statements in the piece is affected by the alphabet format and not logic.

____ Verse 11: This simple statement is at the heart of this whole portrait, "The heart of her husband doth safely trust in her." Modern translations are a bit more clinical about it. Many of them read, "Her husband has full confidence in her."

____ Verse 12: As she may have said in her wedding vows, "I will do you good all the days of my life."

____ Verses 13–16: Now begins the listing of her "chores." She wants to do good for her husband and family. Thus, textile work, scouting out food bargains, and meal preparation—she might even dabble in real estate and plant a garden.

In all of this, she shows good judgment, is industrious, and is in direct line with Lady Wisdom from back in the Solomon sayings. The basis of this woman's quality is found down in verse 30. She is a woman who fears the Lord.

Take Inventory

- Some of us have had the privilege of having young daughters and sons in our homes. Some of you may have them now. Still others are anticipating the fun. One of the difficult moments in child rearing is trying to instill responsibility. Mother's milk and nourishing formula don't necessarily make noble wives and considerate husbands.

To Memorize

Who can find a virtuous woman? for her price is far above rubies.
Proverbs 31:10

. . .

DAY 6

Proverbs 31:17–25

17 She girdeth her loins with strength, and strengtheneth her arms.

18 She perceiveth that her merchandise is good: her candle goeth not out by night.

19 She layeth her hands to the spindle, and her hands hold the distaff.

20 She stretcheth out her hand to the poor; yea, she reacheth forth her hands to the needy.

21 She is not afraid of the snow for her household: for all her household are clothed with scarlet.

22 She maketh herself coverings of tapestry; her clothing is silk and purple.

23 Her husband is known in the gates, when he sitteth among the elders of the land.

24 She maketh fine linen, and selleth it; and delivereth girdles unto the merchant.

25 Strength and honour are her clothing; and she shall rejoice in time to come.

Reflecting on Proverbs 31:17–25

Meaning, please. . .

merchandise is good (31:18) trading is profitable

spindle, distaff (31:19) spinning equipment

coverings (31:22) bed coverings

known in the gates (31:23) respected in the city

girdles (31:24) sashes

Read and React

Her name is not "Wonder Girl" or "Bionic Woman." In many ways, this model woman, wife, and mother is what was expected of the BC female. All of this, without twenty-first-century conveniences.

You will remember that Proverbs 31 came from the pen and library of King Lemuel, probably via the nudges of his mother. This "Wife of Noble Character" was held up as a personification of wisdom. Like wisdom, her worth is "far above rubies." She is her husband's crown (12:4).

Here are her qualifications for "Woman of the Year."

___ Verse 17: She has strength and vigor.

___ Verse 18: She is prudent and attentive.

___ Verse 19: She is diligent and industrious.

___ Verse 20: She is compassionate and merciful.

___ Verse 21: She is courageous and hardworking.

___ Verse 22: She is artistic and beautiful.

___ Verse 23: She is cared for and satisfied.

___ Verse 24: She is a "go-getter" and enterprising.

Take Inventory

- If you are female: If there is a maximum of eight points above in verses 17–24, how many points would you award yourself? What is missing from that list that you, as a contemporary woman, must perform?

- If you are male: What qualifications would you set for yourself to be judged "Man of the Year"?

To Memorize

Strength and honour are her clothing; and she shall rejoice in time to come. Proverbs 31:25

. . .

DAY 7

Proverbs 31:26–31

26 She openeth her mouth with wisdom; and in her tongue is the law of kindness.

27 She looketh well to the ways of her household, and eateth not the bread of idleness.

28 Her children arise up, and call her blessed; her husband also, and he praiseth her.

29 Many daughters have done virtuously, but thou excellest them all.

30 Favour is deceitful, and beauty is vain: but a woman that feareth the Lord, she shall be praised.

31 Give her of the fruit of her hands; and let her own works praise her in the gates.

Reflecting on Proverbs 31:26–31

Meaning, please. . .

looketh well (31:27) watches over
done virtuously (31:29) done nobly
favour is deceitful (31:30) charm is deceptive
fruit of her hands (31:31) the reward that she deserves

Read and React

Thirteen weeks ago we began this enterprise, the study of Proverbs. While there has been lots of repetition and unfathomable imagery, we end on a domestic note that seems just right. Folly and her crowd notwithstanding, this has been a positive experience. Perhaps nowhere else in the Bible can we find such an opportunity to reflect on one's own motives and relationships.

Here we are at the last six stanzas of the hymn to womanhood. We will savor each of them, and add them to the list begun in yesterday's lesson.

____ Verse 26: She is wise and considerate.

____ Verse 27: She is concerned and hardworking.

____ Verse 28: She is adored and praised.

____ Verse 29: She has excelled!

____ Verses 30-31: While grace and beauty may be fleeting, a woman's relationship to her heavenly Father is steadfast and sure. Give her the reward she richly deserves. And what might that be? Children and a husband who will call her blessed and recognition for jobs well done by those who count.

So now, accept this blessing:

The LORD bless thee, and keep thee:
The LORD make his face shine upon thee, and be gracious unto thee:
The LORD lift up his countenance upon thee, and give thee peace.

NUMBERS 6:24–26

Take Inventory

- Wouldn't it be wonderful if each one of us were able to put into action everything we have learned from Proverbs? Perhaps these parting moments should be spent considering that. In light of what you have experienced, what kind of a person ought you to be and will you be?

To Memorize

Her children. . .call her blessed. Proverbs 31:28

Notes

NOTES

NOTES

If you enjoyed

THE EVERYDAY GUIDE TO THE. . .

PROVERBS

be sure to read other

EVERYDAY GUIDE BOOKS

from HUMBLE CREEK

Each book includes a 13-week study, scriptural explanations, and questions for personal meditation. All text taken from the King James Version. 256 pages each; paperback; 5 ⁵⁄₁₆" x 8".

THE EVERYDAY GUIDE TO. . .PROPHECY
Perceptive insights about future things.
1-59310-726-9

THE EVERYDAY GUIDE TO. . .
THE PSALMS
Studies of the Bible's beloved poems.
1-59310-728-5

THE EVERYDAY GUIDE TO. . .
THE GOSPELS
An indispensable guide to the life of Christ.
1-59310-729-3